T0276338

Praise for
*A Brown Girl's Epiphany: Reclaim Your
Intuition and Step into Your Power*

"We need more brave storytellers in this world, and Aurelia Dávila Pratt is one of them. This is a book about stepping into our sacred power, which requires telling the truth about ourselves and the white supremacy that engulfs the world around us. Aurelia's words are a gift to brown women, to remember that you are not alone, and a gift to white folks, to remember that creating a better world requires the work of us all."

—Kaitlin B. Curtice, author of *Native: Identity,
Belonging, and Rediscovering God*

"*A Brown Girl's Epiphany* is a brave and bold invitation to step out of the spaces and frameworks that keep us from our fullness—and to step into our own liberation. With honesty and vulnerability, Aurelia Dávila Pratt takes us on her journey of healing in this powerful and deeply personal debut. It is a sacred gift to us all."

—Kat Armas, author of *Abuelita Faith*
and host of *The Protagonistas* podcast

"When I was five years old, my Mexican mother asked me if anyone ever made fun of me for the color of my skin. I knew I was different from that day forward, and I also knew that being brown meant that I needed to learn how to navigate this world of cascading supremacies. I wish I had this book when I was growing up, so that I knew how to let go of the bullshit and lean into my power. This book is a revolutionary epiphany and will help any of us who are multiply marginalized to step into the divine power that we enflesh. ¡Viva la raza!"

—Robyn Henderson-Espinoza, PhD,
author of *Body Becoming: A Path to Our Liberation*
and *Activist Theology*

"Aurelia Dávila Pratt's work is an offering to the brown girls like me—the ones who heard whiteness tell them they were too ugly, heard society tell them they were too much, heard the church tell them they were too sinful. It is an invitation to let go and to explore the fullness of who we are, where we've come from, and how we want to *be* in the world."

—AnaYelsi Velasco-Sanchez, educator, consultant,
writer, and artist; founder of En Conjunto,
cocurator of the Digital Dine-In Project

"Aurelia's story is as contagious as it is courageous, inviting us to remember and recover our true selves and to come alive to the beautiful mystery within, around, and beyond us."

—Rev. Michael-Ray Mathews, deputy director and
Chief Faith Officer of Faith in Action;
host of the *Prophetic Resistance Podcast*

"Aurelia Dávila Pratt's words are more than an invitation—they are a sacred nudge inspiring the once-silenced, once-small flame within you to burst forth boldly and brilliantly, no longer afraid to shine. If you've ever struggled to trust yourself, to know your worth, or to take up your space in the world, this book is for you."

—Rev. Kyndall Rae Rothaus, author of *Thy Queendom Come*
and *Preacher Breath*; cofounder and executive
director of Nevertheless She Preached

"*A Brown Girl's Epiphany* is the book I wish I'd had when I was a young Latina struggling with my identity. For those of us forced by oppressive systems to disconnect from our racial and ethnic identities, this book offers the opportunity to heal our wounds and affirm our beauty and worth. This book will delight and challenge you as you discover your own epiphanies along the way."

—Karen González, author of *The God Who Sees*
and *Beyond Welcome*

"Aurelia Dávila Pratt writes with honesty, beauty, and courage about her journey. All who give themselves to *A Brown Girl's Epiphany* will find themselves at least a little more whole, discover themselves a few more steps down the road to healing and liberation."

—Greg Garrett, author of *A Long,
Long Way: Hollywood's Unfinished Journey
from Racism to Repentance* and *In Conversation:
Rowan Williams and Greg Garrett*

"*A Brown Girl's Epiphany* is beaming with wisdom and intention. Deconstructing whiteness can be very isolating; Aurelia brilliantly emphasizes the importance of connecting to communities of origin and one's deep-seated knowledge in the whole process. To all the brown women who've been told they are not enough, Aurelia's book will guide you back to yourself and onward to new heights."

—Sandy Ovalle, space-curator, table-setter, creator,
and cohost of *Café with Comadres* podcast;
director of campaigns, Sojourners

"*A Brown Girl's Epiphany* presents unashamed permission to know the strength of our personal stories. Aurelia ushers us into embracing our fullness by the witty and raw insights that help us reimagine how her experience and ours connect to collective healing. Her transparent journey is the timely message we need in the world now."

—Rev. Brittany Graves, spiritual entrepreneur,
all-around advocate, and cohost of *Nuance Tea* podcast

"This book is a treasure. The gift of this book is that by 'seeing' clearly, we are empowered to begin the gritty work of unraveling our own life and to journey toward the loving embrace of the Divine. Aurelia Dávila Pratt's story is also an oasis of rest, refreshment, and recovery of hope."

—Rev. Dr. Isabel N. Docampo, retired,
director of the Latino/a Center for the Study of Christianity
and Religions, and codirector of the intern program,
Perkins School of Theology/SMU, Dallas, Texas

"Aurelia Dávila Pratt has gifted us a book that weaves sacred stories of her childhood into an account of a liberating faith that counters white-supremacist theologies. This work is timely and necessary; it fills a chasm in the literature on the intersection of brownness, biography, and belief."

—Alicia M. Reyes-Barriéntez, PhD, assistant professor
of political science, Texas A&M University, San Antonio

"Aurelia Dávila Pratt invites her readers to sojourn with her toward a deeper understanding of themselves and of God if they are courageous enough to open their hearts and their minds to listen and reflect on what she has to share."

—Bethany Rivera Molinar, executive director,
Ciudad Nueva Community Outreach

"Aurelia calls out the systems and myths that have kept too many of us on the sidelines of our own lives and communities and calls us into the liberating rhythm of abundance. This is the book you want to buy for all the women in your life who are wanting to break out of narratives of domination and step into their own intuition and power. Let the liberating begin!"

—Jennifer A. Guerra Aldana, cohost of *Café with Comadres* podcast and cofounder of Kinship Commons

A BROWN GIRL'S EPIPHANY

A BROWN GIRL'S EPIPHANY

RECLAIM YOUR INTUITION AND STEP INTO YOUR POWER

Aurelia Dávila Pratt

Broadleaf Books

MINNEAPOLIS

For Alicia, Angela, Cosette, and David,
bearers of her smile

CONTENTS

PART 1: STEP OUT OF HARMFUL
PARADIGMS

Opening Words

We are a people who want to be seen and known.
This is a book about seeing and knowing yourself.

We are a people who don't always know how to trust.
This is a book about radically trusting yourself.

We are a people who crave a sense of home.
This is a book about tending to the home within yourself.

We are a people who seek healing and wholeness.
This is a book about the medicine inside yourself.

This is a book about returning to a memory that was always true.
This is a book about us: God within me and God within you.

Introduction

NAMING OUR STORY IS A PATHWAY TO HEALING

REMEMBER WHO YOU ARE

My grandma used to always say, "Remember where you came from." In response to almost any circumstance, she would say it. If I was struggling with some deep tragedy or if I had the audacity to leave an unfinished can of soda on the countertop, she'd happen upon it and snap at me, "Remember where you came from, girl!" It was a command, not a suggestion. So much was unspoken in those simple words, and several years after her death, they continue to go with me. They remind me that our stories matter.

I say *our* because my healing journey is not unlike yours. We are people who want to operate out of our inner fullness. What do we want for the children we love? We want them to grow. We want them to be happy and healthy. We want them to make good choices. And deep inside, we want the same for ourselves.

So to step into our fullness is to believe that there is more to our life than the version we are currently living.

Sometimes we fall out of alignment with this innate desire. We get caught up caring about things that don't matter. We waste our time scrolling on social media, comparing ourselves to others, wanting things we don't have, and treating ourselves unkindly. But in moments of good health, we can see that our fullness is in reach. It is in reach because it is already within us. The ability to make peace with ourselves and to love ourselves well comes from this inner knowing.

Anytime I am operating outside this knowledge of my fullness, my inner voice sounds a lot like my grandma's voice. It sounds like Spirit, speaking deeply into my life, "Remember where you came from! Remember who you are!" I can hear my grandmother's urgent tone; I can feel her fiery passion, and it's as if I am right back in her kitchen taking in a lecture on wastefulness.

My grandma is exactly right. I don't want to be wasteful. I don't want to be wasteful with my life. I want to remember who I am. I want to do this for the sake of my grandmother—for those who came before me. I want to do it for my daughter—for those who will come after me. I want to remember who I am for myself, and I will. I will be a person who operates out of the fullness of my *imago Dei*.

Imago Dei is a fancy theological phrase that means "image of God." It is the idea that we are made in God's own image, and it is one of the most foundational truths about us and God. The message of *imago Dei* is this: We were created in the image of

God. The Spirit of God dwells within each one of us. We don't need permission or any outside authority to access every Divine resource. We already have all we need. Fullness, peace, beauty, liberation: all ours! Unlimited and without condition: ours.

This means we are deeply connected to God, and it also means that we have actual power within us, coursing through our veins. What does it mean to step into our power? First and foremost, it means not to forget that the message of *imago Dei* is true.

Grounding myself in this truth is the stuff my faith work is made of, which is to say it is my life's work. Oh, how I wish I could go back in time and tell little Aurelia all about it. I wish I could save her some pain. But it is healing me now, and it can heal you too.

WHO ARE YOU?

I was in elementary school the first time someone asked me, *"What are you?"* It was a rainy school day in the rural north Louisiana town where I was born and raised. All the kids were sitting in alphabetically ordered lines spanning the walls of the small school building. The teacher on duty had been walking up and down the hallway, when she suddenly stopped and turned to me, asking the question I've heard countless times since.

As with so many childhood memories, I can't remember exactly what was said. But I can remember how I felt. I can remember how my body received the information: shock and confusion, embarrassment and shame. Was something wrong with me?

After this, I became hyperfocused on my brown skin. Did skin color have to do with our family's treatment and overall acceptance in the small town? Was it why we were poor? Was it the reason white parents initially seemed hesitant about my friendship with their daughters? Was this why our neighbor constantly peered out her blinds at us when we moved into her white neighborhood? Was this why my mom frantically called us inside, locking all the doors one Saturday afternoon when the KKK held a public rally in our town square?

Of course, white supremacy did its thing, making me think I was imagining everything. Telling me I was crazy for wondering. For years, it tricked my mind into submission. But as I sift through these stories and ponder how they have shaped me, I realize that I have a lot of healing work to do.

Part of my work is answering a question for myself: not *what are you?* but *who* are you? I am Chicana. I am Filipina. I am the color of the earth. But I'm also more than this. I am a child of God. The stuff of Spirit swirls around within me. I am a culmination of my ancestors' stories. I am a story bearer. My existence is holy, and my healing is their healing too.

NAMING OUR STORY

My grandma used to say, "I didn't cross the border; the border crossed me." She was a product of what her grandparents experienced firsthand when their land was colonized and their culture left on the other side of an unwanted boundary line. "The border crossed me" may have been a punchline, but now I understand the expense at which my grandmother made so many of her jokes. She was a part of a people forced into a new paradigm over the course of generations. It was a culture marked by in-betweenness—no longer fully Mexican but unwanted and unvalued by American society and government.

Because of the liminality my grandma inherited, she spoke a Spanish unique to the borderlands. She was fully Tejana, but she never taught her children the language. Instead, in the late '40s, along with countless other Mexican Americans of their time, she and my grandpa became migrant fruit pickers as a way to travel north.

Chicago is where my dad was born and raised. He is part of a generation of young Latines in middle America who were physically punished if they were caught speaking Spanish in school. White supremacy stole both language and culture from him and his siblings by means of societal assimilation.

My dad married my mom, a first-generation Filipina and Czech Jew, and by the time I was born, they had relocated to Louisiana. I grew up in the late '80s, '90s, and early '00s. The racial tension was never a secret in our town, where most people identified as either *white* or *Black*. There was an unofficial but ever-existing white side and Black side for almost everything: There was a white swimming pool and a Black swimming pool. If a Black kid came to the white pool, everyone stared. Some parents took their children home. And white kids didn't go to the Black pool. Separate white and Black proms were still taking place when I was a kid, and once I got to high school, there was still a white and Black representative for each grade on the homecoming court. There was the white side of town and the Black side of town. There were even a couple of private schools where white families who could afford it enrolled their children—one's mascot is a Rebel, and the school logo resembles the Confederate flag, still to this day.

So even as a young child, it had become clear to me that the color of your skin mattered. From all I had taken in, the message I understood was this: the darker your skin, the harder life would be. Of course, this seemed unfair and wrong even then, but it didn't change the realities I witnessed growing up in the rural South. As a kid, the intricacies of colorism were subconscious and intuitive. It is only hindsight that allows me to ascribe language to it here. I can say now that because I was brown and not Black, I had privilege, meaning I had the ability to benefit from my proximity to whiteness.

When I was young, our family moved into a simple 1,100-square-foot house on the white side of town. From age two to eighteen, I lived in this home. We were the only family of color in the entire neighborhood. As a result, I learned how to speak the language of being white. Regardless of our initial lukewarm acceptance, I learned to follow the rules and norms of a white world. My beloved high-school alma mater was majority Black, but outside of school I lived and moved in a white world. I attended white churches, went to a majority white college, and eventually married into a white family.

For good or bad, I have known and been known in predominately white contexts. I understand this world, and I carry my own set of privileges within it. Still, I've always been aware that I'm not *white* because whether I wanted it to or not, my skin color has always shaped my existence.

CLAIMING MY BROWNNESS

When it comes to matters of race and identity, I have spent the entirety of my life not totally sure where I belong. I have carried a deep shame within me because of my disconnection to my ancestry. When I was a teenager, my sister taught me a trick that we used to gaslight our own shame. If someone spoke Spanish to us, we would say, "Oh, sorry, I'm Filipina!" and if they spoke Tagalog or some other Filipino dialect to us, we'd say, "Oh, sorry, I'm Mexican!"

This only ever happened if we were out of town, because there weren't other Mexican or Filipino families where we lived. Because of this isolation and disconnect with other people like me, I didn't think I had true ownership of these identities. While I didn't know what I was allowed to call myself back then, I never second-guessed whether or not I was brown. The problem was that my brownness was rarely celebrated. Instead, I was most often reminded of it through the microaggressions of insensitive comments or teasing. No wonder it took me so long to embrace my brown beauty, inside and out.

But in 2016, two things happened that woke me up in new ways: I gave birth to my daughter, and Donald Trump was elected as president. Let me tell you, nothing will jolt a brown woman awake like the power of motherhood combined with the glaring white supremacy that marked this presidential election.

Let me be clear: the realities of racism were nothing new, and white supremacy is steeped into the origin of our country's founding. But Trump had a long history of racist controversies, and this knowledge was highlighted throughout the election. I saw this as an opportunity for white Christians to finally talk about racism and soundly reject white supremacy. The grief I felt when white Christians did not show up immediately and without question was eye-opening.

Amid all of this, an ongoing, public dialogue around race was taking place unlike anything I'd seen in my adult life. Black, Indigenous, and brown voices were being centered on the world's stage. They were sharing their perspectives and their pain. They were sharing the truth of what it means to exist in the United States as a person of color.

Through listening to their stories, it became clear that the disconnect I was experiencing in my predominately white Christian context was directly related to my being brown. I had never referred to myself as a woman of color to others before this. I had rarely written and had never spoken publicly about my experiences as a brown woman because I didn't think I had the right or authority to speak. But in 2016, all of this shifted. I finally understood that no one could give me permission to claim the truth of my identity but myself.

In my sermons, interviews, and articles, I began speaking about my brown experience. I did the same in my personal and social media interactions. Even though I continued to struggle with impostor syndrome, I claimed my brownness out loud. Most importantly, I claimed it within me. Embracing my brownness has been the most crucial step I could take toward healing. Finally, with a more integrated self, I came face-to-face with my power and the sacred opportunity to step into it.

OUR PERSONAL HEALING IS A PART OF OUR COLLECTIVE HEALING

We are living in wild times. Political chaos, discord, and divide. Racial tension. Social upheaval. Environmental crisis, economic suffering, and a pandemic that will affect us on a global scale for years to come. Yet none of this is new. It is only an uncovering of what has long been true. The vulnerable were always vulnerable, the suffering always suffering, the poor always poor, and our earth ever mistreated.

How can we move forward amid so much strife? How can we find healing when there is so much pain and suffering to sift through? We absolutely cannot sweep it under the rug. We must face these hard situations and conversations. The only way *around* is *through*. The only way *through* is *together*.

The traumas each of us carries—whether individual, collective, or generational—are all a part of the cumulative pain of this world. But what if the answer to collective healing included personal healing? What if we each did our part by doing the healing work within us? So that we are no longer the walking wounded but instead the fully healed and liberated. What kind of work could we do in the world then? What kind of abundant energy would we suddenly inherit with all those loads off our shoulders?

Many of us have been taught to disregard our stories, but because of this, we disregard our intuition. Many of us have been taught to disregard our intuition, and because of this, we disregard our stories. This disconnect with who we are and where we came from prevents us from stepping into our fullness.

So we name our stories as an act of resistance. We name our stories as a pathway to healing. We name our stories as our contribution to the collective. We do this understanding that it is an essential piece of all our liberation. We name our stories, and through this naming, we find alignment with our intuition, which is to say we embody the truth of *imago Dei*.

This is what it means to step into our power. Yes, it is messy work. It involves untangling ourselves from all sorts of harmful messages. It involves a hell of a lot of unlearning. And it requires our willingness to step into endless new paradigms. Stepping into power is not for the faint of heart. This is why it is so important that we name our stories. This is why it is urgent that we remember who we are.

We are children of God. The stuff of Spirit swirls around within us. We are culminations of our ancestors' stories. We are story bearers. Our existence is holy, and our healing is their healing too. For those who came before us, for all who will come after. And yes, even for ourselves, may it be so.

Part 1
STEP OUT OF HARMFUL PARADIGMS

1

Step Out of
AUTOPILOT

THE NECESSITY OF INTUITION

The path to self-liberation does not have a universal formula, and there certainly is no blueprint for it. Instead, claiming our God given inner authority requires listening to and trusting ourselves. In other words, we desperately need access to our intuition. There's an abundance of resources available to us as we step into this work, from healthy sources of community to art, poetry, nature, and therapy. Regardless of *how* we do it, it is urgent that we begin.

Claiming this part of ourselves is holy resistance because we are soundly rejecting harmful faith paradigms and instead choosing to step into ones that are concerned with our wellness. I believe this is the salvation God wants for us and created us to live into fully! So salvation becomes our choice to let go of what *was* and step into what *could be*. It is new life in the here and now, uninhibited by frameworks that cause harm to ourselves and others. This new life is our liberation! But the fullness of the gifts liberation offers us cannot be accessed without our intuition.

For too long, our experiences have been minimized. We've been told that our hearts will mislead us and are not to be trusted. Instead of being equipped to do our own faith work, too often we are told exactly what to believe and how to believe it. Meanwhile, those in authority conveniently lift up traditions and texts that would preserve their power. *Truth* is spoken of in absolutes without acknowledging that each person's attempt to describe things of God is simply their own limited interpretation.

Stepping into our power means learning to step into all the goodness our intuition will provide us. Simultaneously, it means untangling ourselves from paradigms about God that have kept us bound. This is not a simple chronological process. We are stepping up and letting go all at once. And because intuition is the key ingredient, the process will absolutely look different for each of us. Comparison is not our friend here.

Be encouraged that there is a good place for each of us to begin. We can kick-start the process by turning off autopilot and taking control of the wheel that steers our own faith journey. We step out of autopilot by questioning everything we ever thought was true. This includes the process of deconstructing what we have learned about our faith so far. Here's what I mean by deconstructing: It is tearing down our theological borders and doctrinal fences that aren't just keeping others out but are also preventing us from experiencing the fullness of God in our own lives. It is the work of sacred sifting. It is cleaning up and clearing out unhelpful belief systems and creating anew where necessary. In short, it is unlearning for the sake of the collective, including ourselves.

Many of us have been tethered to certainty for a long time when it comes to matters of faith. We need black-and-white answers to carry on. *Either/or* thinking has helped us feel safe and secure. This stifles our ability to extend compassion to ourselves and others. It also puts God in a tidy box that never opens or changes, which ultimately limits our access to Divine encounters.

Learning to step out of autopilot is unsustainable without a posture of nonduality. We must strengthen our faith, not through answers but by finding comfort in the gray areas. This involves mastering the art of holding things in tension. Granting mystery space must become our most fervent spiritual practice. Father Richard Rohr describes nondualism in this way:

The dualistic mind is essentially binary, either/or thinking. It knows by comparison, opposition, and differentiation. It uses descriptive words like good/evil, pretty/ugly, smart/stupid, not realizing there may be a hundred degrees between the two ends of each spectrum. Dualistic thinking works well for the sake of simplification and conversation, but not for the sake of truth or the immense subtlety of actual personal experience. Most of us settle for quick and easy answers instead of any deep perception, which we leave to poets, philosophers, and prophets. Yet depth and breadth of perception should be the primary arena for all authentic religion. How else could we possibly search for God?[1]

When we learn to embrace nondualism as a part of our faith posture, we are committing to our own freedom. We are setting aside the way of easy answers given to us and instead choosing to follow the path of authenticity. Of course, this path is more work. It is certainly the harder way. But it is the path most in alignment with our *imago Dei*. And because of this, we not only have permission to travel it, but we are empowered to do so.

I wish I had known about this when I was a child. But the truth is that I did know about it. Children naturally understand this nondual posture. We see proof in their attention to wonder, their radical acceptance of what is unseen, and their unlimited imagination. These characteristics are Divine gifts, yet kids are swiftly encouraged to dispose of this innate wisdom and fall in line. For many of us, our churches and the power of church culture in our communities were a driving force behind our disconnect from intuition.

RECLAIMING INTUITION AFTER RELIGIOUS TRAUMA

I grew up brown and Catholic in a predominantly evangelical context. The Catholic presence in my town was so small that a priest from another parish had to drive in every Saturday afternoon so that we could receive Mass. My young mind lamented, *Does this really have to be another thing about me that is different?* Most of my peers were Baptists, and so I would often attend youth group events with them.

Because being Catholic was not the norm in my community, I was often teased about our noncontemporary music and the liturgy, and I was accused of worshipping Mary. Mostly, I was told over and over again that I wasn't a Christian. The latter happened all the way through college. I was so boggled by this because I knew I had what the Baptists liked to call a personal relationship with God. Yet I was told by children and adults alike that it wasn't valid if it didn't fit their formula.

In college, I was rebaptized in order to join the Southern Baptist church where I had become heavily involved. Prior to my rebaptism, I had a serious conversation with one of my mentors because I was conflicted about invalidating my original experience. Somewhere down deep, my intuition was telling me another baptism was unnecessary. But I was told my Catholic baptism didn't count, and I believed it.

Around the same time, I signed up for a two-month mission trip in the Philippines. Let me go ahead and make it clear that the Aurelia today would not sign up to go overseas and save the poor brown people! But regrettably, the Aurelia twenty years ago believed it was her God-given duty to evangelize others into the Christian tradition. Mission trips were all too common in the Southern Baptist world, and because I was a good Christian girl, I signed up for these trips any time I had the chance.

Having grown up in such a rural part of the United States, I had never traveled so far away. But my maternal grandfather had been a Filipino immigrant, and so I thought this trip could be a beautiful opportunity to connect with a part of my heritage. When I arrived, I realized the area's demographic was almost entirely Catholic! I didn't understand why we were going door to door offering Bibles and tracts, trying to convert people away from an already-Christian faith tradition.

I found the courage to approach the main missionary with my questions and concerns, and yet again I was told that Catholics weren't Christians. He even sat me down and went through the Bible to prove it. I'll never forget how it felt to be so young and alone in a foreign country as this powerful man quite literally looked down on me, disregarding my experience. What had brought me here if not my love for God? Yet I was so deeply disconnected to my intuition that I didn't have access to my power, much less my voice. So I swallowed my pride and assumed my instincts must be wrong.

And yet, even now, all these years later, my Catholicism continues to be a part of my faith that sustains me. I am not talking about a church tradition, a set of beliefs, or even a community. I am speaking of the mystical faith of my childhood. It is the wonder-filled, imaginative faith of my child self, before all the indoctrination set in. I knew God intimately in this place. I had access to my intuition. I had not yet switched on the autopilot required of me.

THE ROLE OF SACRED COMMUNITY

The irony is that I would eventually become a Baptist pastor myself, albeit not the kind one might typically imagine. Still, I bring my story along with me, hopeful that it will shape the way I lead and reimagine sacred community in a post-church world. My work context is a rarity and the primary reason I have continued in church ministry. I have total freedom to do my own faith work: freedom to deconstruct, question, and evolve. I am free to do all of this beautiful work within my community, as a part of the community.

Because our leaders are able to authentically navigate our faith, we have been able to create an environment where the entire community can do the same. Deep in the heart of central Texas, we have managed to create a small oasis of people, many of whom were done with church until we found each other. This is relevant to our work of rejecting an autopilot kind of faith. As clergy, I must acknowledge that I am a part of a legacy of faith leaders who have doled out the ways people should believe, encouraging them to swallow whatever they are spoon-fed.

This is not what people need from faith leaders. It is not what they need from a sacred community. People need space to hurt. They need space to heal. Most of all, people should have space to evolve and expand. And at times, I have learned that many people need healing outside of church and how important it is to bless them, not judge them, as they go.

The end goal of a sacred community shouldn't be to keep people in the fold. Our hope should be the same for everyone: that each one of us would fully experience the peace of God both directly and consistently, whatever that may look like. Wherever it may be.

The fact is that people are rapidly deconstructing right on out of the church doors. When this happens, those who decide to stay should send them on their way with love and support. Mostly, we should understand that this is all a part of the holy task of switching off our autopilots.

Sacred community can be extremely valuable and healing. But at the end of the day, there is no pastor, mentor, or friend who can do our faith work *for* us. They can support us. They can walk alongside us. They can bear witness to our growth. But, ultimately, we are responsible for our own faith journeys. And we cannot step into the fullness of our power without choosing to navigate them for ourselves.

DECONSTRUCTION AND DECOLONIZATION GO HAND IN HAND

I mention sacred communities because they can be one way (though not the only way) for us to become practiced in thinking about our collective oneness. This is important because we don't step out of autopilot simply for our own sake. We do it for the healing and wholeness of all creation, ourselves included. Our inner work is a part of this larger work. Stepping into our fullness will always be incomplete without tending to the *imago Dei* of the other. Collective liberation should always be our end goal.

When we fully accept *imago Dei* within us, we begin to recognize it in everyone else as well. And the need to assess our personal beliefs and practices becomes a stepping-stone in understanding our contributions to harmful systems. As we wake up to our personal modes of autopilot, we notice a need to deconstruct, but deconstruction will only get us so far. We must also do the necessary work of decolonizing our faith. The two go hand in hand.

Some of us may be able to get through deconstruction with our faith intact, but decolonizing will not let us off the hook so easily. It will present us with the truth that Christianity is a whole hot mess. It will require us to reckon with how the Bible has been used as its weapon of mass destruction. With that sacred text in tow, Christianity spearheaded the domination of stolen land from Indigenous peoples in our country and across the world. It placed its blessing upon slavery. And it continues to perpetuate violence against women, the queer community, and the earth itself.

Acknowledging these hard truths is not a rejection of our faith but an embrace of it. It is finally seeing the fullness of *imago Dei* in all of God's creation. So we decolonize.

We decolonize whenever we question the narratives we inherited and elevate the voices of those historically on the margins of society. We decolonize whenever we actively untangle ourselves from systems of oppression and embody the necessary reparations. We decolonize our minds and our lives by opening our eyes to the harmful faith paradigms we've unknowingly embraced. Like Christ on the cross, we lay down every defense. We let the necessary deaths happen. We do not look away. Why would we? The opportunity for new life is often just around the corner.

MOVING FORWARD WITH OUR INTUITION IN TOW

Once we turn off our autopilot, we will see reality for what it is: a bundle of paradoxes. One helpful paradox will be the work of going back and going forward. We go back in order to reclaim our intuition for the journey. For me, this looks like reclaiming the faith of my childhood. I have to go back to before I switched on the autopilot. I believe this is the posture Jesus was speaking of when he told us to be like little children. Again, going back to this place requires a lot of unlearning and deconstruction, but it also means we get to reimagine and create anew.

Simultaneously, we must move forward into healing. For me, I have needed to move forward by finding people and communities who engage faith in a way similar to me. While no one else can do this work *for* me, I also know I cannot learn to trust myself if I lack the safe environment to do the hard work involved. Having kindred souls in my life who are on a similar journey is what makes this difficult work sustainable. I don't have a prescription for what community should look like for others. I only know we weren't meant to walk this road less traveled alone.

Turning off our autopilot is the kind of thing we will have to do again and again. We never *arrive*. Rather, we acknowledge this sacred work as a spiritual practice. So we practice, and then we practice again. We question. We wrestle. We sit in the muck of the mystery. We realize that certainty isn't all it was cracked up to be, and we let it go. And then we do it all again.

2

Step Out of
SHAME

THE SHAME IN MY NAME

One of the most significant shame sources in my life is my name. I love my name. My parents named me Aurelia (*Latin for "golden"*) Joy. My mom even inscribed in my baby book the words *"Aurelia Joy: a golden ray of light who will bring joy to the world."* These words have been a prophecy and a blessing that continue to speak into my life in powerful ways. And yet I have a lot of trauma around my name as well.

Growing up in rural north Louisiana, it seemed as if nobody could say my name without struggle. I remember my dad calling me over to the sidelines on my first day of t-ball practice. "The coaches are having trouble with your name. Tell them to call you Rae-Rae," he told a five-year-old me, citing my family nickname. Fast forward nearly twenty years later, and this intimate term of endearment was still being watered down for the use of acquaintances. I was working at J.Crew as a personal stylist, but I was struggling to make commissions because no one could ever recall my name. I started using Rae as a way for people to remember me. This nickname, originally reserved for family and close friends, was once again handed over to strangers who couldn't make the effort to pronounce my real name.

Back when I was a cheerleader in high school, an upper-classman often disregarded me. I had rarely felt someone's energy and body language so strongly. It told me, "You are not worth my time or energy. You are not valuable." There were several instances when she explicitly made these sentiments clear. At one of my first practices as a freshman, she called me over with an eyeroll, casually saying, "Hey, *Uh-ray*" (her version of a shortened "Aurelia"). Then she said, "By the way, I'm just gonna call you '*Uh-ray*' because your name is too long." I don't remember what was on the other end of her request, only the part where I wasn't worth the extra two syllables.

After high school, I attended a university forty-five minutes down the road from my childhood home. I would cringe during roll call on every first day of class. Hunched down in my seat, dressed in dark colors so that I didn't stand out too much, I would wait in a state of panic for the inevitable pause. The professors almost always paused when they got to my name as they considered how it might be pronounced. They would eventually stop the roll call completely to ask me to pronounce it for them in front of the auditorium full of students. They'd jot down a quick note and continue on. No one seemed to mind, but I would be on pins and needles and sweating with anxiety.

I hated this moment that occurred in almost every class I took, and it began with freshman orientation. There were hundreds of people in the assembly area for a brown-bag lunch the school had provided. During the lunch, a representative from a local bank gave a talk that included a fifty-dollar raffle prize. I've rarely had luck with raffles. But, of course, on *this* day, as the man drew a name out of hundreds of incoming freshmen, he paused with a perturbed look on his face. My stomach sank. He proceeded to gloriously butcher my name, and everyone had a laugh. I grabbed my fifty bucks and rushed back to my seat, eager for anonymity once again.

What's ironic is that I technically pronounce my own name incorrectly. I rarely thought about how I was pronouncing it when I lived in Louisiana. I have always pronounced it the way my parents spoke it to me (*uh-ray-lee-uh*), telling others, "It's pronounced like Arabia but with an L." But ever since I moved to Texas well over a decade ago, people have been telling me at every turn that I am saying my name wrong. I've been told by colleagues, at the gas station, in the Costco checkout line, by the cashier at REI, and more. Over time, I've become increasingly self-conscious when I say my own name.

I don't mind when people call me by my name in its traditional Spanish pronunciation (*aww-rail-ee-uh*). I love the sound of my name in Spanish. What I mean is that I've been *corrected* over and over again. I've been told that I am wrong for how I say it. This cord of shame handed to me is just one of many complex layers tied around my name.

SHAME BUTTONS

The shame around my name lives on the surface as an exposed shame button that anyone can press. When this happens, it elicits an immediate trauma response. But this source of shame runs much deeper than the pronunciation of my name. Because I grew up physically and emotionally disconnected to my racial and ethnic identities, it took me a long time to understand this. My deepest source of shame lies in the fact that I don't speak Spanish. Because of this, I have held on to a fear that I will always exist in a liminal space. Like a lot of people, my shame is rooted in a yearning to belong.

This lack of language is an ever-present source of shame that causes me to question the claim to my own identity. It also keeps me bound to traumas I need to let go of, such as the racial traumas prevalent in my childhood and adolescence. I have unconsciously told myself that these experiences are what validate the truth of my identity where community has not. Ironically, they are also in large part why I am so disconnected from the language of my ancestors in the first place.

I think about the racial slurs that have come my way in the form of jokes over the course of my life. My heart sinks knowing that the majority of the time, they came not from bullies but from people I considered friends. I think of how people have spoken about "Mexicans" degradingly right in front of me, in both childhood and adulthood. The moments are too vast to recount here. And did I ever speak up for myself? Never. Instead, I swallowed the jokes and crude remarks with a painted-on smile, shock coursing through me. I cloaked myself in the shame of it and dissociated from my identity as a way to survive.

I wake up to all of this, and, my God, it fills me with grief. At the same time, I can hear my grandma snapping at me, "Remember who you are, girl!" My identity cannot be rooted in shame any longer. And as I sift through my traumas, I realize I don't need the shame anymore. It does not serve me. It cannot help me. It cannot come with me on this journey. My identity is grounded in the truth of *imago Dei* and the power it continues to provide for me.

The same is true for you. You and I, we are the same. We are image bearers. We are children of God. Divine light radiates from within us. Power dwells under our surface. But we are bogged down by shame that is tethered to our traumatic experiences. Perhaps we cannot undo the traumas. But, damn it, we can reject the shame.

TRAUMA IS SHAME'S OLDER SISTER

Shame keeps us from our fullness because it prevents us from enjoying our lives. It binds us to mindsets of guilt and fear, separating us from our intuition. We tighten shame's hold on us when we raise our kids and navigate our relationships and careers within the same paradigms. Shame burdens all of us, keeping us bent, unable to stand in our power.

We cannot fully grasp our inner authority when we are entrenched in shame's grip. Getting free is an easier-said-than-done kind of work, though, because we are both recipients and participants in shame's bidding. We inherit cords of shame from our traumas and our contexts. From our own wounded-ness, we even pass them out ourselves. However unintentional it may be, the impact is the same: we are bound. We must acknowledge the relationship between shame and trauma so that we can untangle ourselves from the narratives they culti-vate in our lives.

Trauma is shame's older sister, taking its cues from what it has seen play out already. Shame mimics our trauma triggers like a little sister playing copycat. It highlights them like a kid wearing their sibling's hand-me-down clothes. Shame is what causes us to go back to a wounded place over and over again.

But I am learning: sift through the trauma and move in the general direction of healing, and shame will have one less thing to cling on to.

OUR INTUITION IS ALREADY GUIDING US

I have this memory from high school in which my white boy-friend came to pick me up for a date. Back then, I used to wear white tank tops ("wife beaters," we called them; thanks a lot, patriarchy) with a colorful bra underneath. My friends and I thought we were so cute sporting this style. I remember walking out feeling so confident on this day, when my boyfriend looked me up and down disapprovingly and said, "What are you wearing?"

I responded with resolve at first, but then he said, "I can see your *brown* nipples." It wasn't just what he said; it was also how he said it. It was the look of disgust on his face. It was the way his tone changed and his lips curled down when he said the word *brown*. A shockwave of humiliation coursed through my body as I registered what it meant that he included this adjective in his displeasure. I didn't just have nipples showing. I had *brown* nipples showing.

This is just one small example of what it is like to live every day in a brown body. In fact, it's actually pretty incredible that I held on to this particular memory above so many others. I'm positive he forgot about it minutes after he said it. I'd bet he had no understanding of his own racist undertones. I'm sure he hasn't given a second thought to the harm he threw my way that day. But I never forgot. His words were daggers of shame that penetrated my body.

For a long time, this is what I remembered about that day: how he handed me a cord of shame, which I freely accepted and wrapped around my body with the rest of them. So when I speak of untangling ourselves from shame, I really mean it. We have to name the shame. We have to identify the traumas that inform it so that we begin unwrapping ourselves from shame's hold on our lives.

This is painful work (and sometimes it requires professional help), but at least in this case, it turns out that remembering the shame was more useful than harmful to me. Because I named the memory, I also remembered something else. I remembered that I didn't change what I was wearing that day! I did not change out of my see-through shirt that showed my nipples. My irreverent nature, passed down from my grandmother, showed up and out in that moment. I am laughing as I write this. Hooray for young me! I am cheering her on so hard right now.

My intuition carried me in this small act of resistance, even as my body received a message that harmed me. My defiance saved me even when I didn't have the words to verbalize the truth behind what was happening. It wouldn't be the first time, and it wouldn't be the last. This is a powerful reminder that my most sacred God-given resource is not something I have to acquire or even become. My intuition is already guiding me.

Our intuition is already guiding us. Do we need to wake up to it? Perhaps. Do we need to connect more deeply to its voice? Always. As we move away from trauma and untangle ourselves from shame, we find something beautiful waiting, offering us sustenance for our journey: courage. Our courage energizes us, empowering us to move into the healing places we once feared. As we move into these healing places, we also move toward a deeper connection with our intuition, which is the essence of our *imago Dei*.

It is this self-trust that is the stuff of belonging. It starts from within. I know there is only one person who can give me the permission I need to live fully into my existence. That person is me. This is in large part why I am doing this work and writing these stories. I write with compassion and an unlimited well of love and tears for my younger self.

The same is true for you, my friend. You can look upon your former self with understanding and love, knowing that they didn't know the things you do now. You can grant yourself the permission needed to step out of shame's hold and into the fullness of your power. And you have the guts to do it too. I know it because you already have what you need. Your intuition is *already* guiding you, and you have every blessing of *imago Dei* going with you. It's yours. Like a gift, you only have to accept it, open it up, and use it.

3

Step Out of
HIERARCHY

YOU AREN'T UGLY; YOU'VE JUST BEEN AROUND TOO MANY WHITE PEOPLE

In the summer of 2020, there was a meme going around on Instagram that said, "Do you remember when you first realized you weren't ugly; you were just around too many white people?" As soon as I saw it, memories began rising to the surface.

As a little kid, I don't remember ever feeling pretty. Some of it was probably tied to the fact that I wore chunky glasses and sported uneven bangs from a young age. Some of it was my family's inability to afford things many of my peers could. Some of it was cultural, like how my mother wasn't privy to the norm of (white) mothers buying their (white) daughters a collection of bows that would hang on a long strip in their bedrooms. It felt like a status symbol for little girls. Most of it had to do with the color of my skin, and the shame ran deep: I believed I was ugly.

I thought I was ugly in the photos taken on the last day of second grade. All those spring to early-summer recesses in the hot sun had added up, and my brown skin was extra dark. Sandwiched in between two white friends, I am smiling big after a fun day. At that moment, I was filled with laughter and happiness. But the photo was developed weeks later, and when I saw it, shame rocketed through my little body as I compared my brown skin to the fair skin of my friends.

In the fourth grade, there was a girl in my class who everyone adored. She had light skin, golden hair, and a sweet smile. Every morning, when she would arrive, all the girls would run to her, yelling her name in excitement. Every morning, I perceived that the standard of beauty was the opposite of me.

My older and wiser sister assured me this wasn't true. She promised me that one day I'd see. She repeated something my grandmother would often say to us, "White people lie in the sun every summer in order to look like us!" But I took none of this to heart. They might want to be tanned, but they certainly did not want to be Mexican.

My assumption was proven to be true in middle school when a group of white boys teased me relentlessly. Any time I walked by or stood out in any way, they would yell out the name of a Mexican pro wrestler accompanied by derisive laughter. Filled with shame, I wanted to hide under a rock. For years, any time I told someone about this, they would use patriarchy's favorite dismissal of girls to assure me that these boys treated me this way because they liked me. But I don't remember being flattered by their treatment. I do remember how it felt to be publicly shamed daily because of my skin color. I remember wearing dark colors and attempting to be quiet whenever they were around. I remember going home every day after school and crying.

In junior high, I ended up dating a white boy from another school who didn't tease me for the color of my skin. I went to church with him every Sunday night for two years. I loved that little church and many of the people in it, but the lighting was terrible. It was bright and harsh, and I hated how it emphasized the contrast of our skin tones when we held hands during each service. I remember feeling dirty and ugly as I compared them.

The way our relationship started didn't help. He was worried that his parents might not approve because a relative had told him that the two of us dating went against the Bible. At the time, interracial dating was extremely taboo and unacceptable in our town. It was a scandal that reverberated across the community anytime someone dared to defy this unspoken law. When my boyfriend's parents decided it was okay for us date, their response was, "But only because she isn't Black."

I'll talk more about colorism in just a bit, but here it is again: the reality that my *brown-but-not-black* skin resulted in proximity to white (albeit, half-assed) acceptance. Just writing this story down, I have to stop to take some deep breaths.

I feel endless rage for every Black and brown child who grows up with this blatantly racist messaging normalized. For every microaggression that seeps into their little bodies over time, I am likewise filled with anger. And I grieve for every kid of color who continues to experience their fullness stripped from them as they grow up. I wish I could protect them from these inevitable realities. I wish I could alleviate my own shame that caused me to feel ugly for much of my childhood. If only I had understood the layers of systemic racism rooted in the language of all our hearts.

ENGAGING THE BUZZWORDS

As we do our inner work, we begin to see how many of our wounds are caught up in a larger web of hierarchical systems. We are all connected, and we must become a people who think about healing with all of us in mind. None of us can step into liberation fully as long as others are still prevented from doing so.

Moving toward this collective liberation involves thoughtfully engaging important language. Doing so is a crucial entry point into our healing work because we gain understanding of how hierarchy affects all of us. Here are a few common buzzwords, defined:

> **White supremacy** is the social, economic, and political systems that collectively enable white people to maintain power over people of other races.

> **Dominant culture** the group whose members are in the majority or who wield more power than other groups. In the United States, the dominant culture is that of white, middle-class, Protestant people of northern European descent.

> **Colorism** the prejudice or discrimination against individuals with a dark skin tone, typically among people of the same ethnic or racial group.

Antiracism is the policy or practice of opposing racism and promoting racial tolerance.

Patriarchy is a system of society or government in which men hold the power and women are largely excluded from it.

Feminism is the advocacy of women's rights on the basis of the equality of the sexes.

By grounding ourselves in the definitions of these terms, we are able to acknowledge the existence of these forces and movements. However, filtered through the funnel of political rhetoric and social media interactions, the truth of these concepts gets muddled. Instead of honestly engaging them and assessing how they are relevant to our lives, people often toss them out as unhelpful buzzwords.

Instead of throwing out the buzzwords, we need to make room for them. Making room looks like listening to the experiences of people of color. It means believing women when they voice abuse or mistreatment. Making room means throwing out theology that harms LGBTQIA people or rejecting policies that harm the most vulnerable.

By choosing to make room, we are participating in a collective conversation and movement toward healing. All of us would be better off without white supremacy. Each of us would be more whole without the harms of patriarchy weighing us down.

However, we cannot change as a whole without liberating our individual minds and hearts. Understanding how our stories and experiences are a piece of the larger whole is a part of our inner work. We do this uncomfortable work so that we can step outside the harms of hierarchy and choose another way.

BEAUTY AND BLOW POPS

Growing up, I lived close to our local high school, and so every Friday night, I could hear the football announcer from my house. Under the light of the stars, I would dance to the sound of the band and drumline. My sister, Alicia, was a high-school cheerleader, and I wanted to be just like her. So I would pretend all night long. The energy from the crowd, the sounds and smells all fueled my imagination. Blocks away, the moment was mine.

One Friday night when I was ten years old, I got to be at the game in the flesh. Even better, I had some quarters. It was just enough to purchase one Blow Pop from the concession stand. I remember walking down the bleachers, around the corner, down the wheelchair ramp crowded with people coming and going. I crossed under the bleachers where the band sat, past the stadium entrance and the booster club selling spirit ribbons. Finally, I reached the concession stand.

I picked one of the half dozen lines, excited to purchase some candy, which we hardly ever got at home. When it was finally my turn to order, a Black woman greeted me with a smile. I proudly handed her my quarters and asked for a Blow Pop. She nodded and walked off to grab it. When she returned, she had two in her hand, and she handed me both, my eyes widening in surprise and confusion. Her smile reached her eyes, and she said to me, "Here's your Blow Pop, and here's an extra one for being so pretty!"

This is the first memory I have of being called pretty. This Black woman spoke into my life in a way I would never forget. Whether she realized it or not, she named my brown beauty when I couldn't. Even now, the memory of that interaction is healing. Her words felt like solidarity. She saw me. What power! This woman planted a seed of knowing within me that night: my existence was beautiful. Unfortunately, it would take time for that seed to take root.

ACKNOWLEDGING COLORISM

Growing up, the loudest voice I heard was that of white supremacy. The message it regularly sent me was that my brown skin was inferior and ugly. While this tore me down personally, it also instilled colorism within me. Engaging the reality of colorism is a part of my healing work because it helps me understand the ways I benefited from being brown and not Black in my context. It's important to differentiate my brown experience because the color of our skin (including the shade of our skin) affects our lived realities. This acknowledgment helps me identify the parts of myself that perpetuate colorism in my beliefs and actions today.

I seek to understand how my wounds are connected to the whole because my liberation is tied to collective liberation. My racist experiences are not unique, and sadly they are only the tip of the iceberg of what it means to exist in a brown or Black body. I've certainly experienced trauma, and my healing matters. At the same time, my personhood has never been seen as a threat. My life has never been in danger because of the way I look.

I am reminded of this daily as Black and brown people continue to be killed by the police, while white mass shooters are taken into custody with a level of dignity unafforded to people of color. Just in the span of writing this chapter, Derek Chauvin has received a guilty verdict on all three counts of his murder of George Floyd. Daunte Wright, Adam Toledo, Ma'Khia Bryant, and Andrew Brown Jr. have all been shot and killed by police. All instances were different, and yet none was different: to be Black in America (and, in Adam's case, brown) is to be perceived as a threat, even if you are a child.

I was texting with a close childhood friend, who is a Black man, while all of this was happening. We have a shared understanding of the rural southern context we grew up within while acknowledging our experiences were very different because of our skin colors. Talking about everything happening now, my friend told me, "Some days I don't even want to go outside. They are killing Black men out there. Who's to say I'm not next? But then again, they are killing Black folks in their apartments as well. So what are my odds?"

I hate that his words are true. I hate that there's nothing I can do to immediately change his reality. Sure, I know what it's like to feel ugly because of my skin color, but I'll never know what it's like to be feared. I may know what it's like to feel inferior, but I'll never know what it's like for my existence to scare people. I'll never have to consider every move I make as if my life depended on it.

Through my own encounters with racism, I know a fraction of my friend's feelings and experiences. I could never know the fullness of what it means to be Black in America, but I know enough to understand that my healing is not sufficient. As I open my mind and heart, I see with urgency a need for systemic change. Our collective liberation depends on it.

WE MUST REJECT HOW POWER IS DEFINED

Christianity has long been its own hierarchical system, using harmful biblical interpretations to sustain its power and suit its own needs. Colonization of Indigenous lands has been called "ordained by God." Slavery has been justified and upheld. Violence against women, the queer community, and people of color continues, and the earth is dominated rather than stewarded. When Christianity is seen through this hierarchical lens, we all suffer.

Christianity, when propped up with the image of a white male God, hurts all of us. It uses dogma to mass manipulate, keeping us tethered to harmful ideologies. We are taught not to trust our own bodies, voices, or experiences. We are taught to be dualistic thinkers who never ask questions. Shame is used to keep us from faith-wrestling, which prevents us from accessing beautiful things like nuance and mystery. Over time, we learn to stifle our impulses. If we cannot, we risk disrupting our relationships and losing our community.

Christianity's cultural influence spans across political and social norms. Because it is such a powerful force in the United States, its effects touch all of us, including those who don't identify as Christian or attend a church. Even for those who have found healing through progressive Christian interpretations and communities, it is still a struggle to untangle ourselves from the ways Christianity causes harm.

Christianity has been like Big Pharma. It profits off of keeping us sick, meaning it benefits when we are disconnected from our intuition. There will always be exceptions, but too often, it requires our constant self-denial in order to nourish its hierarchical roots. This is a problem, but we are not without hope.

When we are listening to our own God-given Spirit, we inevitably become in touch with our power. From this place, we are less concerned with doctrine and prescriptions. We are less prone to be force-fed theology or manipulated into embracing paradigms that harm us or others. We are less likely to prop up systems of hierarchy and more likely to follow the way of love.

Jesus showed us how this liberation work was done because his entire existence was a rejection of how power is typically defined. In his pinnacle teaching of the Beatitudes, Jesus flips the notion of power on its head. Where we lift up status, reputation, and wealth, Jesus blesses the poor, the grieving, the meek, the merciful, and the peacemakers. Jesus redefines power by teaching a liberative posture grounded in love and humility.

This is how to shine. This is how to be light. This is how to be. This is why the way of Jesus is valuable and relevant. Besides his words of wisdom, Jesus lived a life that was true to what he believed. He lifted up the vulnerable. He centered those on the margins. He made space for the voiceless. He doled out miracles to those in need of healing. He embodied his own teachings beautifully, believing so strongly in the vision of heaven on earth that he died in solidarity with it.

The story of his resurrection can be our call to live resurrected lives too: lives that rise beyond the status quo. Lives that are in alignment with Spirit in us. Lives that redefine power by leaning into the nonhierarchical paradigm of Christ. There is room for all our healing, and all our healing matters. This healing is rooted in our joint existence, and so our self-liberation depends on us making this shift: we must become people who think about the collective.

4

Step Out of
POLITENESS

UNMIND YOUR MANNERS

Our self-liberation journey is full of paradoxes. It is about
looking inward *and* outward all at once. It is deeply personal
and also macro-minded. So It's not enough for us to digest
the empowering parts of this process only to reject the tricky
moments of discomfort and self-scrutiny. We must sift through
our place in it all.

This is why systemic problems matter and are relevant to
our inner healing. I want to shout from the rooftops how much it
matters! I want to yell out how we are all connected! But I can't.
I can't yell. It wouldn't be . . . polite.

My family migrated from the northern United States to rural
Louisiana just before I was born, so I grew up in a household
with significantly different norms than the families around us
that had long-established roots in the South.

In elementary school, I learned the hard way what happens when you do not say "ma'am" or "sir" to your teachers. I remember being so confused by the appalled expression on my teacher's face as she scolded me in front of everyone for my bad manners. I wanted to explain to her that I didn't know, I wasn't practiced, and I honestly forgot these rules and messed up sometimes. Eventually, it sunk in that the norms were different outside of our home, and I learned to mind my manners at all costs.

Now, as a matter of great urgency, I am learning to unmind them.

WHITE SUPREMACY IS THE CRAZY EX-BOYFRIEND

I often refer to white supremacy as *the crazy ex-boyfriend* because it's real and it's harmful, and yet I often question myself instead. Disoriented from its mind games, I've wondered time and again, *Am I imagining this experience? Is something wrong with me?*

For many years of my life, I assumed this was the case. But when I listen to Black and brown voices, I hear stories that validate my own. Slowly but surely, I am finding the strength and the support to get out of this abusive relationship. Now, when it comes to matters of racism, I choose to listen to the experts: those directly harmed by it. Black people, Indigenous people, and people of color are the only ones who can truly define racist experiences.

Yet white supremacy uses politeness to put a bow on racism. It keeps us all in line so that we cannot fully call out the abuse it inflicts. Our bruises are kept hidden, covered up by the rules of polite society. This minimization and acceptance of everyday microaggressions ultimately lead to disproportionate violence toward Black and brown bodies.

What this means is that *believing* the experiences of people of color is a crucial part of our healing work. This is why something as small as the function of politeness really isn't so small at all.

A SACRED PAUSE

Several years ago, I was leading a church meeting. We don't own our own building, and at the time, we were worried about a timing conflict with our gathering space. At some point, I made a joke related to the situation. I knew each person in the room and felt safe being lighthearted in a tough spot. But later I received an email in which someone expressed their concern. *What if we would have had visitors that day?* They were worried what I had said might seem unreflective of the love of Christ.

As I was crafting my apology email, I hesitated. My instinct told me that in this case, my actions were less about being Christlike and more about fitting under the umbrella of politeness. My understanding of politeness has been primarily informed by a white southern-hospitality sensibility, and it has always been a bit triggering for me. Suddenly, it made sense to me: I realized I'd been trying to fit under this damn umbrella my whole life and that I was shrinking myself in the process.

So for the first time I could remember, instead of automatically apologizing for my too-muchness, I paused. This sacred pause was just enough for me to change my usual course. Instead of sending my email right away, I thought about other friends of color, wondering if they'd ever had similar questions. I also thought about my family. In these contexts, how I spoke in that church meeting wouldn't have been considered rude by a longshot. Of course, reading the room can often matter, and understanding the cultures of individuals, groups, and organizations is invaluable. But why does what's acceptable and unacceptable so often seem to be set by the same people?

I asked several friends and family members if "white and polite" was a thing: "Is it just me? This sense that I need to be prim and proper and nonoffensive based on the definitions set by southern, white Christians? This feeling that my existence is too loud? That I need to filter myself?" I rarely thought to question these norms before. I just always assumed something was wrong with me. I'd often navigated this struggle in isolation, but this time was different. Every person I contacted responded, not only affirming me but also sharing their own stories.

Once I realized I wasn't alone in my experiences, so much began rising to the surface. I had questions about things I'd never thought to question before. I started waking up to the ways I had doubted myself, limited myself, and second-guessed myself. I began to notice the many ways I tried to change myself to fit a particular mold of what a woman should be.

As a brown woman pastor in a male-dominated field, I have lost count of the times I have apologized for being too much. I have spent so much precious energy filtering my fire and quelling my nature. These parts of me that are beloved reminders of my grandmother, parts of me that have helped me survive, I have tried to quiet again and again. But in the sacred pauses, I choose to remember the truth about myself.

You can do the same. In the uncomfortable moments of listening and reflecting. In the inevitable seasons of inner upheaval and faith crisis. And in the effort to understand your interconnectedness to the whole of creation. In the sacred pauses—those holy in-between spaces—remembering the truth of your *imago Dei* will equip you for this journey.

WHITE AND POLITE

The politeness construct keeps all of us small. For people of color, the necessity of code-switching steals our energy, keeping us from our fullness. I call it "white and polite" not to offend, but because in my honest experience, white people don't often recognize the ways they set norms around politeness and then expect the rest of us to follow suit.

The power of politeness cannot be ignored. Honesty is often reframed as contentious, and vulnerability that isn't "positive" is upsetting. Anger or pain caused by racism is often shut down because these expressions don't fit the politeness narrative. Because the act of pointing out microaggressions is dismissed as impolite, people of color are often disregarded when sharing their experiences. This not only makes the healing process traumatic, but it also makes racial reconciliation nearly impossible.

In the Bible Belt, where I've spent my entire life, the concept of politeness is often rooted in Scripture, whether through the "fruit of the Spirit," the definition of love, or the concept of peacemaking. With the politeness narrative, we are sent the message that love is conditional based on our performance, and that peace means never rocking the boat. Patience means waiting for the other side of eternity to experience equity. Kindness means never speaking out of turn and always watching our tone and manners. Self-control means stifling every vulnerable or rage-filled emotion.

Essentially, politeness becomes a surface-level biblical interpretation, reducing our Spirit work to little more than pious performance. This is antithetical to authenticity, which is a key ingredient to our fullness journey. But when these concepts are practiced with thoughtfulness and depth, our interactions with one another can be radically transformed.

Love becomes a deep desire for our neighbor's liberation. Joy becomes delight in creation's thriving. Peace moves from passive to disruptive for the sake of justice. Patience becomes the stamina to bear witness to each other's pain. Kindness becomes our willingness to make way for what is true, no matter how uncomfortable. Generosity is a decisive shift from scarcity living to nonhierarchy embodied. Self-control becomes our willingness to set aside ego tendencies and make sacrifices for the sake of our collective healing.

I am a big appreciator of politeness when it is not used as a placeholder for our actual work in the world. Unfortunately, it is too often used to cover up the realities of white supremacy. Acknowledging this can be our first step out of shallow-end swimming and into the deep end.

I LAUGH SO I DON'T CRY

Around the age of nine, I attended summer camp with some of my friends. At the end of the week, achievement certificates were distributed in front of the whole camp. I was filled with excitement at the thought of winning something, but my excitement quickly turned to disappointment when my name was called out. I was given the Sunny Disposition Award, and I had no idea what "disposition" even meant! I walked up to receive my certificate with a confused smile.

Back home, my sister explained to me what it meant to have a sunny disposition, and she assured me that it was a great award. I didn't appreciate it at the time, but later, I was able to recognize that I had indeed been born with an extra dose of joy.

Honestly, I'm not sure I could have survived some of my circumstances without joy and humor to see me through. To this day, I am one of those people who laugh at inopportune times. I laugh as I'm sharing uncomfortable news. I laugh when things are quiet or awkward. I smile even when I'm sharing hard truths.

The more I consider it, the more I believe this is a trauma response. I laugh so that I don't cry. I laugh at myself before others can laugh at me so that reality doesn't hurt so much. I joke to make light of my own painful experiences.

I used to take my light-haired, light-skinned nieces on outings, and I would make the self-deprecating joke with a laugh: "Everyone probably thinks I'm the nanny." A few years later, I gave birth to a light-skinned, light-haired baby of my own. She is the spitting image of her dad. And one day on a trip to the aquarium, it actually happened. I was mistaken for her nanny.

I walked away from that encounter in shock, trying to make sense of what had just happened. I did the thing you do when you're a person of color in an abusive relationship with white supremacy. I thought of all the ways to excuse it. "I look young," I told myself. "Maybe too young to be a parent?" (I was thirty-two when this happened.) "It's in the middle of the week when people are usually working," I thought to myself later. "Maybe she thought the parents would be at work." "She didn't have bad intentions," I reasoned. "Her assumptions were not mean-spirited."

I have been groomed by white supremacy to question myself when I am the recipient of inherently racist microaggressions. I shouldn't have to explain how this is racist, and yet white supremacy forces me to go back into my trauma again and again. If I choose not to laugh along with it, I am required to explain myself.

So here it is: were mine and my daughter's skin tones reversed, I would not have been asked if I was the nanny of my child of color. No, others would have certainly assumed that I adopted this child. I would have been seen as her white savior. But I am not white. I am brown. Therefore, I am easier to envision as a nanny than as a mother to a white child.

RAGE

I have noticed a common occurrence among white people when I speak out about the truth of microaggressions. Their reaction is akin to rage. People are very uncomfortable in the presence of my honest thoughts. People are unsettled, and usually they react in the form of aggressive energy directed at me.

What I have noticed among my peers of color is that I am not alone in this. The effort to be fully seen and heard doesn't often feel worth it. There is only so much energy we have to devote to trying to get people to see and acknowledge the truth of our experiences.

What's ironic is that I recognize the anger directed at me because a quiet rage also burns within me. It is a rage inherited by the generational pain of being a woman of color. Every once in a while, it finds its way to the surface. But most often, waiting to greet it is either vilification or total rejection.

I realize this is not a sustainable way to live. I want to remember all of who I am *before* rage. I want to know who I am as intended by the Creator. I want to be grounded in these truths. I want to stand in the legacy of my ancestors' beauty. I want to fully exist.

The more I untangle myself from hierarchical systems, the more I understand how the construct of polite society keeps me from doing this healing work. Its unrealistic expectations harm all of us. And the thing is: you and me, we are capable. We are smart enough and nuanced enough to sift through what's helpful and what's not.

In order to step into our fullness, we need to examine the ideas around politeness and step away from the ones that ultimately cause harm. And there's nothing to worry about in rocking this boat because there's never any danger in becoming *more* thoughtful.

Doing this work won't make us any less kind or less mindful of others. Instead, we are likely to become *kinder, more* mindful, and *more* genuine because our hearts and minds expand the deeper we dive in. Every time we rethink a previously unquestioned norm, and every time we make space for our intuition, we are doing it. We are gaining momentum. We are finding ourselves again.

This is what it means to live into fullness. It is to seek to be expanded and then to fill those expanses up with the truth of our *imago Dei*. And so our fullness is good. Mine and yours. *Good*. We are doing the work of stepping into our power. We are finally beginning to understand how much more we were born to be. No strings attached. No unneeded pressure. And no bullshit rules that don't do anything but keep us small.

5

Step Out of
PRODUCTIVITY
CULTURE

FLOW, NOT FORCE

My community does this radical thing where we don't have
a Sunday service once a month. We call it *Feed Your Soul
Sunday*, and every first Sunday we encourage people to do
something that gives them pure uninhibited joy. Because, let's
be honest: for many of us, church is no longer it.

Even though my copastors and I were nervous to pitch this
idea, it was well received and is now a beloved fixture within
our church culture. We rest. We rest because we are a small
community, and everyone shoulders some part of the work. We
rest because our pastors are multivocational, and the traditional model of worship was not sustainable without leading to
burnout.

We rest because when we assessed our particular needs (rather than comparing ourselves to how church is "supposed" to be done), we realized that a regular Sunday off would help us thrive. We rest so that we have more energy to create opportunities for deeper relationships. In short, we rest because we are interested in reimagining sacred community outside of the constant need to produce.

Ever notice how miserable we all are trying to live up to the impossible standards of productivity culture? There are so many downsides. We are busy. We are tired. We are discontent. And worst of all, we are disconnected from our bodies and the earth. Countless methods and books and training programs are all designed to help organizations instill a culture of productivity in their workplace. Yet this is the exact paradigm we need to examine and step out of on our healing journeys.

Productivity culture sends us the message to deny ourselves and ignore our needs until we don't even know what they are anymore. It is why we struggle to know and listen to ourselves. It's part of why we need to be on this journey of remembering who we are in the first place. We are constantly pushing through to produce. We are pushing through, trying to keep up, until the next small breather. We are only surviving. It's not enough.

When the world tells me to push through, my response has become *"flow, not force."* Pushing through sucks the joy out of everything. Pushing through makes it seem like it's admirable to suffer. But I have no desire whatsoever to suffer if I don't have to. I don't think we were created to intentionally drain ourselves dry or make ourselves miserable.

Flow, on the other hand, is Spirit movement, and it is happening with or without us. Our job is not to create the flow. Our job is to notice it and jump in. Our job is to pay attention and to honor what we hear. We can become people who daily choose flow over force.

I'm done pushing through. I want out of that contract. I'm stepping out of this rigid relationship with productivity and time. I'm stepping into flow instead, which means I'm listening to my body, paying attention to energy, and building the foundation for the kind of "home" I want to dwell in.

The home within ourselves is our ultimate safe place. It is where each of us is fully *us*, where our *imago Dei* is front and center. There's so much about our lives that we cannot control, but we get to decide what our inner home looks like. We get to decide what comes out of it, and we get to decide what—or who—comes in. When our house is in order, the rest of our lives can flow out of this abundant source.

Flow, not force. We may not always have the ability to change our realities or circumstances, but we can decide how to proceed in good health despite them.

ASTROLOGY AND ROUTINE

My friend Brittany and I have a podcast called *Nuance Tea*. Through it, we are venturing outside the boundaries of typical Christian themes and letting curiosity guide open and honest conversations. We are exploring. We are disregarding unspoken rules and stepping into alignment with our truth.

As I write this, we are deep into our first season, exploring topics including energy work, trauma, grounding, and rituals. We recently recorded an episode on astrology. We talked about how the influence of evangelicalism has kept us from tapping into astrology's healing resources. We talked about the power of collective energy and how our attention to creation (in this case, the sun, moon, and stars) offers us guidance and power. We read our natal charts and delved deeper into who we each are.

As Brittany was reading my sun sign, Sagittarius, everything she was saying was spot on. *Yes*, I thought. *I am bold. I love to laugh and tease. I'm friendly and enjoy being around people.* But then she said something that made me laugh out loud because it was so unlike me: "You disdain routine," she read.

Ha! Anyone who knows me knows I live for a routine. Brittany knows how much I love routine, and she laughed too. She knows how intently I've been investigating my relationship with time. She knows I've discovered it's a huge source of my anxiety and how part of my healing is transforming my relationship with it.

As I do this work, I take comfort in the fact that I am not unique. Many of us are overdone by the realities of our daily lives. Meanwhile, the endless stream of information on the internet reminds us that the world desperately needs our care and attention too. We are pushed and pulled every which way just trying our best to cope, and time does not seem to be our friend.

THE PUZZLE PIECES IN MY HEAD

I often visualize my anxious mind as a puzzle. When I'm in my rhythm and everything is in order, the puzzle pieces in my head all fit together nicely. No chaos. No mental gymnastics. Everything is in sync.

When I experience change or upheaval, my puzzle breaks apart, the pieces knocking into each other like bumper cars, trying to find their fit. My mind furiously attempts to piece them back together. I struggle to relax if my puzzle is not in place. But irrational thinking clouds my judgment, and I can't see clearly. Over and over again, I get the puzzle wrong. It takes extra time and energy to find a rhythm that enables my puzzle pieces to fall back into place.

At any given moment, I'm tending to the puzzle in my brain. It may require less energy when I'm at home, in my rhythm, but it is still there. It's the reason I struggle whenever plans change unexpectedly or if I'm traveling. Anytime unknown or unexpected variables present themselves (which is everyday—ha!), I have to redo my puzzle.

I wish this weren't the case. It certainly isn't rational. But it doesn't matter. Anxiety isn't rational, yet it's a very real experience. And when my puzzle comes apart, it is anywhere from exhausting to debilitating to tend to it.

Sometimes I'm able to use coping skills, and sometimes I need medication. The best way I have learned to manage my daily anxiety is through order and structure. If I can know what to expect, then I can function mostly normally. So I lean on routine and schedule as if my life depends on it. This would be just fine if I existed in a bubble by myself. But I have a daughter, a partner, relationships, and a job. All these moving pieces require the ability to be flexible and to take changes in stride. My struggle to do this has revealed an unhealthy relationship with time.

But as I do my inner work, its healing effects permeate all areas of my life—even my relationship with time. The more I step into this work, the more I discover my intuition. The more I trust my intuition, the more I am able to listen to my body. The more I honor my body, the more natural it feels to follow its rhythm over the rigidness of time and productivity. The more at peace I am with myself, the less concerned I am with an intact puzzle. The less anxiety controls my life.

Any mental illness is specific to the individual. While the intuition journey is similar (deeply personal and without a universal blueprint), choosing to take the journey will ultimately produce some form of healing results. Head, heart, and body in tow, this is the kind of production we should get behind.

THE ROLE OF EMBODIMENT

Like most humans, every week I wash loads of laundry, which then need to be folded and put away. It's a no-fun, grown-up task alongside working, parenting, cooking meals, and tending to side projects and other chores. And nearly every week, I get it done.

But some weeks, my body tells me no. Instead, it tells me to get my ass to the TV! And for me, a creature of habit, saying yes to this prompt is radical. Why? Because my physical and mental and emotional self is asking for rest, and I am saying yes. I am treating myself kindly by honoring my body's requests.

The more I listen, the funnier the messages have become. One day, half an hour before a Zoom meeting, my body told me to go take a bath. I really needed to prepare for the meeting, but I decided to listen to my body instead. I cannot tell you how relaxed, confident, and prepared I felt going into that meeting. The hot water provided a place to step back, unplug, take a breath, and begin again. When I entered the space of needed productivity, I was more equipped.

Another time, I was significantly behind on my weekly sermon. Yet one morning later in the week, I found myself tending to my plants. At first, I kept thinking about how I really needed to go to my office and get to writing. But eventually, something deeper within me—a voice I haven't always had access to—calmly and firmly told me, "No. This is where you need to be. This is what you need to be doing." So I surrendered to that present moment of watering, trimming, tending. And soon after, I found myself running for pen and paper. I ended up jotting down the entire sermon all in one moment!

Bit by bit, I am deconstructing my relationship with time. And I am creating new boundaries, beloved walls for my inner home. I am doing this by quite literally rejecting what I'm supposed to be doing a lot of the time! As much as I've been able, I have begun listening to my body over my to-do list.

Listening to our bodies and allowing them to help us navigate our way through time is an essential part of reconnecting with our intuition. As our relationship with time evolves, the more natural it will feel to reject the rat race of productivity culture.

TOUCH THE EARTH

At the start of the COVID-19 pandemic, I told my dad how anxious and stressed I was managing the realities of a new normal, alongside tasks that still had to be done. His wise response? "Take a moment or more to just breathe. Touch the earth. Find grounding."

I took his advice. I went outside, and with bare feet I stooped down, touched the earth with my hands, and breathed in deep. Although my circumstances didn't suddenly change, I felt a sense of relief in those few quiet moments. I was reminded of my connection with creation and of all our Oneness. And I experienced renewed energy to keep going—as well as the power to believe I could.

Deepening our relationship with the earth is another way we can let go of the pressures of productivity. Grounding practices that involve nature, such as going on daily walks, have become a sacred practice for me. Spending time with my hands in the dirt through composting and gardening has helped me develop a more contemplative lifestyle. Meditating with the elements, and understanding my kinship with them, has filled me with humility and gratitude.

All of this has naturally changed my relationship with time. I'm less anxious when I'm spending time with the earth. I feel less urgent about things. I have a better sense of my priorities. These practices have been medicine to me. They fill me up, compelling me to keep up my work while boldly reframing what it looks like to do it.

From a place of groundedness, we can more clearly see the harms of productivity culture. We can also identify our own ability to make small changes in our lives that will loosen its grip on us. Remember, we may not be able to control our circumstances completely, but we get to decide on our own posture. We get to decide what our inner home is like.

AMBITION

As we opt out of productivity culture, we do not leave our ambition behind. There is an important place for ambition in our lives. We need it as we do the bold work of stepping into our power. We need it as we shift from timelines informed by our woundedness to timelines informed by our God-given Spirit-intuition.

Spirit-timeline does not work at the same pace as our hurried, scarcity-driven egos often do. It is not concerned with productivity, expectations, or other people's opinions. It is not worried about resources or opportunities running out. Spirit-timeline produces abundance.

When it comes to our work, our creative projects, our relationships, and whatever other roles or responsibilities we have, we can choose to operate on our Spirit-timelines. We can find peace with the progress we are making at our own pace and in our own time. We can be at peace with the season we are in, even as we move forward with a healthy dose of ambition.

Our relationship to productivity shapes our attachment to scarcity mindsets. It feeds off of our individual and collective traumas. But in stepping out of it, we gain healing tools such as how to protect our energy, set boundaries, rest, and honor the time we have in alignment with our bodies. We also gain access to our own Spirit-informed ambition, which fuels us on the journey.

We filter all of this through the realities of our lives, offering ourselves unlimited self-compassion along the way. Compassion is essential because we aren't meant to disengage. Rejecting productivity culture doesn't mean we aren't productive or even disciplined. It only means that we've reclaimed our hold on time in a way that strategically energizes us so that we can face the fullness of our realities head on. Yes, it's hard as hell. Yes, there is so much we cannot control or change. Yet somehow this truth also remains: our pathway is *abundance*, and we were created to walk in it.

6

Step Out of
SCARCITY

HOMEMADE WRAPPING PAPER

I grew up with my family initially intact, which included my
parents and two older sisters. My oldest sister struggled with
several mental health diagnoses, which kept her in treatment
centers for much of my childhood. My mother left our family
when I was ten. And my middle sister, traumatized by family
dysfunction and our town's racism, joined the military and got
the hell outta Dodge as soon as she could. By the time I was
twelve, it was just me and my dad.

When I was a baby, we lived in a small house on one end
of town. On that side of town, my sister had almost been kid-
napped one day while she was outside playing. On another
occasion, a man (who would end up robbing and assaulting a
woman down the road) had tried to force his way into our home,

but my mother was able to keep him out. Later, she would have to pick him out of a lineup and testify against him.

So when we moved to the shag-carpeted 1,100-square-foot home in a decent part of town, it was a huge step up. My dad worked hard hours for years in order to move us into that house and create some kind of a life for us. We didn't have much, but we never went without food. There wasn't extra money for outings, the newest toys, or the dance classes my friends took, but our basic needs were always met.

Still, growing up around kids who could afford to buy and try new things, I often felt insecure about our situation. These children went on *family vacations,* for goodness sake. Every summer! They *went places.* Meanwhile, I was learning my place in this little town, based on my skin color, whether I liked it or not. I *already* had a laundry list of experiences with unbelonging. I didn't like being different in this way too.

For a long time, I made scarcity-driven decisions rooted in these childhood traumas. On vacations, I like nice hotels, a concept totally foreign in my childhood. I want to pack however much I want without worrying about taking up too much space. And I want to buy things new, even though second-hand shopping is friendlier to our environment. Basically, adult me often wants what my child self didn't have access to.

I used to be hard on myself and feel guilty about this, but now I understand that feeling limited is triggering for me. Thankfully, knowing means I can understand the connection between my childhood experiences and my current choices. Knowing means access to some much-needed self-compassion.

Knowing my posture means that I can adjust it. *Knowing* makes all the difference.

One year, I got invited to a birthday party at the skating rink. Of course, our tiny town didn't have fun things like skating rinks. But the next town over did, and I was invited! It was one of those parties where the whole class was invited. Well . . . everyone *white* in the class was invited. The fucked-up, unspoken rule was that outside of school, you didn't mix races. I lived in a white neighborhood, and I wasn't Black. So I got an invitation.

But there was a problem: we couldn't afford both a tube of wrapping paper *and* the small gift my mom had picked out at the store. I couldn't show up to the party empty-handed, so my mom used her artistic skills to fashion a paper grocery bag into wrapping paper. She even decorated it beautifully with her own hand drawings. It turned out gorgeous. Naturally, I was mortified.

I cried in humiliation, imagining myself walking into the party with homemade wrapping paper. I begged my parents to *please* (just this once!) buy this extra thing. But to no avail. I was a little brown kid who was also highly anxious, and I was going to a party where I sensed I didn't fully belong. On top of this, I was going to practically announce to everyone that we couldn't afford things as small as wrapping paper. I couldn't bear it.

I don't remember skating, but I do remember being ushered to the private room—the one reserved for people who could afford to invite half the class to their birthday parties. I remember the dread I felt as the birthday girl was handed gift after gift while we all watched. And I remember shrinking in my seat as she was handed my simple gift, the one made out of a grocery sack.

As she looked at it, she paused, her eyes adjusting after the previously extended trance of furiously opening packages. This gift was clearly not like the others. She took it in silently. Then she squealed in delight. She showed her mom. She showed the children around her. She announced to everyone, "Look at this! It's so pretty. It's *homemade!*"

WE CAN REWRITE OUR NARRATIVE

Here's what I wish: I wish I'd been born with the confidence and vision to understand that my mom's homemade wrapping paper was awesome. I wish it hadn't taken the validation of others. I wish I hadn't cared about what anyone else thought of me or my family. After all, this kind of caring was the beginning of losing touch with my intuition.

That gift with the rad homemade wrapping paper was a display of our lack of wealth. I have no idea if other people saw it that way, but I saw it that way. That gift was wrapped up in what we *didn't* have, and I was wrapped up in what we didn't have as well. Only my adult self can understand what I missed out on in that moment: I missed the gift my mother had given me as she poured hours of time and love into that paper bag. I missed appreciating the art that was created out of her efforts. I missed an opportunity to participate with her: to be creative. To lean into originality.

This is what scarcity does. It keeps us from recognizing and experiencing beauty.

I know I'm not alone. Most of us are wrapped up in scarcity mindsets that tell us we are in constant danger of loss, whether that loss is related to our people, our time, or our stuff. We want good lives, inside and out, but scarcity is the antithesis of fully living. It is hypothetical living. It is halfway living. It is almost but not quite living.

Scarcity is the sense of foreboding when you have dared to embrace the goodness of life. It is the embodiment of "what if." Scarcity is being stuck in a place of pain. It is being afraid to move. When something good happens, scarcity is always waiting for the other shoe to drop.

Scarcity is allowing trauma instead of healing to inform us. And it's not our fault that we are often bound to it. We've needed this way of seeing the world for our own survival and protection. But as we move into healing, we realize that scarcity is not for us. It does not reflect the fullness of who we are, and we have permission to rewrite our narratives without it.

HEARTBREAK

When I was ten years old, my parents divorced, and my mother moved back up north. She'd live with her parents, go back to school, and start over. Ironically, that moment I missed with my mom and the wrapping paper would be one of my last opportunities to bond with her. My sense of scarcity would be cemented by the wound of her leaving.

I always felt close to my mother. Like next-level close. Even at ten years old, I clung to her, and she doted on me. She'd play with me, listen to me, run my bath in the evenings, tuck me in every night, and sing to me. To my young eyes, she was perfect. My favorite person. Then she was gone.

It's taken me years to parse out exactly what happened. I've had to piece events together with my sister. The trauma runs so deep that I blocked a lot of it out. I can only remember bits and pieces: My dad telling me about the divorce at his office after work one day. My mom staying out late and being home less often. Finding out from my sister that Mom gave custody to Dad. Crying myself to sleep on the couch that night and waking up with an ink stain on my favorite jeans. Coming home from school one day to discover she had left Louisiana and was headed back to Chicago. My grandma's harsh tone to me and my sister: "Don't cry for your mother. She doesn't deserve your tears."

Here's what I know now: My mom did the best she could with the resources and emotional capacity she had. My mom was operating out of her own trauma. I may not have a close relationship with my mom, but she has always loved me. I have compassion, empathy, and forgiveness for my mother.

But here's all I knew then: My mother left permanently, and she didn't say goodbye. Even after she was gone, she listened to my cries over the phone, and they weren't enough to bring her back. I didn't know if or when I would see her again. So this is the trauma my young body received: the impossible possible. An unquestionable presence suddenly absent. My first heartbreak.

FROM SCARCITY TO ABUNDANCE

The pain of abandonment created a sense of scarcity so deeply ingrained in me that I can hardly understand my identity apart from it. Scarcity has told me that love can run out, security can run out, safety can run out. It's all conditional. When scarcity shapes how I proceed, I operate out of fear, anxiety, insecurity, or codependency.

There are endless forms of scarcity-living, but it is almost always rooted in our traumas and adverse life experiences. Something we feared was proven true. Or something caused us suffering, and our survival instinct is to prevent that suffering from happening again. And our scarcity mindsets add up. They contribute to our collective posture.

Our society operates out of scarcity more often than not. We are grown-ass people who don't like to share. This is reflected in our immigration policies, in our health-care system, in our obsession with guns and violence. Scarcity drives us to jealousy and comparison. Scarcity compels us to hoard our resources and our platforms. Scarcity keeps us from centering other voices. Scarcity tells us there isn't enough power or status or success to go around. And scarcity convinces us we don't have the ability to face the nuances of life or to deal with hardship and pain.

We mindlessly live from this place, all while abundance is within our reach. Unconditional abundance that is not attached to what we do or don't do. Abundance that is not attached to our circumstances or our bank accounts. Abundance that is our birthright as children of God. We have the power of *imago Dei* making up our DNA, coursing through our veins, making our bones strong. Filling us with Spirit. Offering access to every Divine resource. Holy capacity.

THE GIFTS OF RESILIENCE

Our inner work must include the task of sacred sifting. We sift through our thought patterns, our spiritual practices, our daily rhythms, our relationship tendencies, our financial choices, and so on. We sift out everything informed by scarcity, understanding that this will not include every decision that is rooted in trauma. Trauma has caused us suffering, and it has kept us from healing. But our trauma has also given birth to resilience, which has granted us some gifts along the way. What are yours?

Here are mine: Yes, I want to overindulge as a result of my childhood experiences. But I am one of the most giving people you will ever meet. Resilience granted me abundant generosity toward others *and* myself. Yes, my experience with abandonment may have shaped me into a person who deeply fears being alone. But in good health, I can sift out the unhelpful relational patterns and simply be a person who is loyal AF. Resilience has gifted me with thoughtfulness and loving kindness. Forgiveness is one of my superpowers, and I'm a ride-or-die friend.

I could give so many more examples, and I know you have many too. As we sort through the trauma, we've got to drop our limiting mindsets while taking the gifts of resilience with us. We are sacred sifters, dropping scarcity like it's hot and taking everything good with us.

ROOTS

One summer, my copastors and I created a retreat for the kids in our community. For one activity, we facilitated a meditation that was taken from my favorite children's curriculum. It speaks a message of Divine abundance we could all use. The meditation asks you to imagine yourself as an extraordinary being with roots, wings, and tentacles.

> *Your roots are attached to a source that gives you energy, vitality, strength, and courage. That source is God's love. Imagine your roots like open tubes pulling vast amounts of that love, tons of it, into your form. Fill up your roots and your form. Now use your wings and fly anywhere you choose. Where you go, you spray that love from your roots through all the little tentacles in your form. When this love is sprayed out, it takes on different forms. Go to a place anywhere in the world that you care about. Spray it with love. What does that love look like? (Pause.) Remember, God's love can never be exhausted. So make sure your roots are open and you are refilling your form.*[2]

When we are living in alignment with our *imago Dei*, our posture is one of abundance. We understand that every Divine resource is available to us: peace, hope, goodness, joy, creativity, and so on. These resources root us in Divine love, and they never, ever run out.

From this place, we can be secure in the knowledge that we have all we need to embody healing in our daily lives. When we embody healing, we embody wholeness. We embody beauty. We embody the truth of ourselves.

Part 2
STEP INTO
YOUR POWER

WARNING:
Stepping into your power
is not for the faint of heart!

Your effort to *become*
will first require an emptying.

When honoring this truth,
you will disrupt unhealthy patterns.

When finding your voice,
others may try to silence you.

When choosing your healing,
some will lash out, terrified.

And you may feel betrayed
by ones you love.

Old wounds will rise up;
new ones will present themselves.

Listen.

The beauty, the growth,
the gifts—

your expansion
is worth it.

So resist
the urge to shrink.

Resist
the urge to stop.

Resist
the urge to rethink.

Allow resistance
to be your entry point
and forward motion
your dearest friend.

Finally,
let intuition guide you.

Step in, step in.

7

Step into
ABUNDANCE

OPEN HANDS

Several years ago, I scheduled a therapy session to work through anxiety rooted in my mother wound. Namely, I was terrified to have kids. I was ready to try, but my fears were overwhelming me. So I sat down in a room with a therapist I had just met and laid it on him. Bogged down by the *what ifs*, I named fear after fear:

> What if I can't get pregnant?
> What if something happens to my husband?
> What if my anxiety is so debilitating that I'm unable to parent well?
> What if I don't really know myself, and I'm capable of leaving?

The therapist listened patiently before offering a response. Finally, he said, "Notice how none of the *what ifs* is hopeful.

None of them wonders about good futures. This is because those *what ifs* aren't from you. They are your anxiety speaking to you, but they aren't *you. You* have the ability to reframe the *what ifs.*" Then he said to me:

"What if you give birth to a beautiful baby?" (I did.)
"What if you are an incredible mother?" (I am, damn it!)
"What if you have a wonderful life with your partner?" (Pretty amazing so far.)

None of our *what ifs* is guaranteed. But the act of choosing to believe good things over our lives is a shift from ego scarcity to the abundant hope of *imago Dei.* We can choose to believe we have every emotional and spiritual resource needed to face all the realities of our lives. Yes, we risk disappointment, grief, and failure. But we also open ourselves up to goodness we previously didn't have the capacity to entertain.

Now when I catch myself worrying or feeling anxious, I will usually discover that I'm also holding my breath, my body is tense, and my fists are clenched. So when I practice reframing the *what ifs* that inevitably flood my head each day, I have to take my whole body with me in breaking out of it. I do this by taking deep breaths, relaxing my body, and loosening my grip. This embodied act of surrender is the capacity-creator needed to shift my way of thinking and doing.

Daily I reposture myself this way because here's what I'm learning: tight grips leave no room for abundance, but open hands are a Divine invitation.

THE RISKY BUSINESS OF DREAMING

In order for us to step into abundance, we must become people who are willing to dream. Many of us have quieted our urge to dream as a form of protection. Yet we sense ourselves growing out of this restricted existence. We need more. We deserve more. To nourish our roots, expand, and flourish, we require all that is beyond scarcity living. Embodying this belief is called *dreaming*, and it is a vulnerable and courageous business.

Growing up, the world I knew didn't provide much imagination for dreaming. Our limited resources made dreaming seem like a privilege I didn't have access to. On top of this, patriarchy told me I was vain and selfish to dream, while white supremacy told me I didn't fit the mold. These things resulted in imposter syndrome, which told me over and over again that I wasn't worthy of dreaming. So instead I used a mixture of bad theology and platitudes to navigate decision-making. I would tell myself that the right doors would open at the right time. Then if something didn't work out, I would tell myself it was a shut door and call it a day.

This worked for a long time. Until I outgrew it. Until it occurred to me that I was letting people and systems off the hook by operating this way. Until I realized I was minimizing my intuition and downplaying my labor. Until I understood that this kind of existence was out of alignment with my *imago Dei*.

As I peeled off the protective layers of scarcity I had wrapped myself in, and as I dared to dip my toes into the waters of abundance, I had an epiphany: I could listen to Spirit within me. I could trust myself. I could open the doors I wanted to open and create the tables I wanted to set. I could create the reality I want to see.

Even while so much is out of our control, we can decide on our reactions, on our way of thinking, and whether or not we are living in Divine alignment with our *imago Dei*. We can take this risk. We can dream. Doing so is one of the most radical acts of self-love we can offer ourselves.

THE WILD DREAMING OF JANN

When I was thirteen, a series of traumas and tragedies brought a beautiful soul into my life in the form of Jann. My oldest sister and Jann's youngest daughter were close friends. When Jann's daughter tragically died, Jann came, even in all her grief, to comfort my sister.

Over time, I developed a friendship with Jann as well. It was certainly unexpected, but Jann became a mothering presence I needed at such a pivotal age. I will always consider it one of life's sweetest gifts that I got to know her.

Jann was a master artist as well as an arts educator and reformer. She had a family, a career, and a beautiful life of her own. Yet she invested in me! I look back on the love she freely gave to my younger self, and I am overwhelmed with gratitude.

Though Jann lived a state away, she showed up for me again and again. She cheered me on in my softball games and school plays. She helped get me ready for school dances, saw me through all my teenage heartbreak, and even took me along on some of her travels, enabling me to see bits and pieces of the world for the first time.

Jann wasn't any ordinary person. She was a bona fide wise woman with an aura of joy that radiated around her. She could light up any room like a sunbeam, and her voice was filled with kindness. Jann was the embodiment of authenticity. She was incredibly down to earth, and yet she was also wrapped up in heaven. Ideas dropped into her lap in abundance. She was so *connected*. To creativity and love. To the beauty of life all around her. Everyone—*everyone*—loved her.

Jann effortlessly perceived the needs of others, going above and beyond to approach every situation with understanding and empathy. She was the kind of person who would refuse to use the handicap stall of a restroom just in case someone else actually had need of it. She always made sure she had cash on her in case she encountered a person on the street asking for money. Once, I parroted something I had heard about homeless people and asked, "What if they use the money you give them to buy drugs or alcohol?" Jann said to me, "What if they don't?"

Jann was teaching me to reframe my *what ifs* before I even realized it. And out of everyone in the world, it was Jann who taught me about being a woman and a good human. I still can't believe my luck. It was Jann who taught me how to navigate my emotions and honor each of them. It was Jann who taught me to see the beauty in my skin. She taught me that beyond my small town, there was a whole world and way of being for me to discover. She taught me to dream.

It's been a dozen years since cancer took Jann, wrenching her away from countless loved ones one week before her sixtieth birthday. It's been a dozen years since I said goodbye to my dear friend at her bedside, a dozen years since she offered me the mothering presence I hungered for. And yet even without Jann here to physically guide me, I am still learning from her. I am still telling her story. I am still honoring the ways in which she wildly dreamed.

A RECIPE FOR DREAMING

Jann was a dreamer. It was as if there was an open channel between her and heaven in which creativity and every other element for dreaming flowed. She had an unending openness to new ideas and different kinds of people. She possessed emotional, spiritual, and physical persistence. She prioritized playfulness. Her attention to beauty was so deep it felt like a prayer. Radical kindness and generosity were her offering to the world.

Through all this, Jann left her lasting imprint: a recipe for dreaming that the rest of us can tap into via our own authenticity. Jann effortlessly embodied creativity, openness, persistence, playfulness, attention, kindness, and generosity. We can access these same ingredients, not by striving to be like Jann or anyone else but through the radical act of being ourselves. The more we embrace our *imago Dei*, the more we trust ourselves. The more we trust ourselves, the more we consistently lean into a posture of authenticity. Our authenticity equips us in our dreaming. It paves the truest path for each of us, which is a path no one else can lead us to, except ourselves.

I am learning that the practice of dreaming *in and of itself* produces abundance. It is healing work that results in its own set of growth gifts. Even if I don't achieve or receive whatever actual fill in the blanks I had hoped for, the fact that I am *willing* to dream sets me on an alternate trajectory.

I mentioned earlier that I have a podcast with my friend Rev. Brittany Graves. *Nuance Tea* has been a practice in dreaming for us. For me, it's been a way to create the reality I want to see. The work of it has required me to change my usual patterns. I've had to change the way I spend my time to make room for it. I've had to pour my creative and financial resources into it. I've had to be disciplined as I learn new skills such as editing and producing. I've had to be vulnerable each time we've shared a new conversation with the world.

I love using *Nuance Tea* as an example of dreaming because it's more than an idea. It's something Brittany and I have put time and energy into; we've stayed authentic and open in the process, and we have seen a vision come to fruition because of it. At the same time, we are not yet a widely known show with sponsors, a large social media platform, or sustainable monetization. Regardless, endless returns have been found in the investment we've made toward our vision. This foundation we are laying represents a willingness to lean into abundance and to continue showing up in this posture day after day.

The inner permission and confidence this act of dreaming has provided me have transformed me and expanded my mindset. It's given me courage to make changes in other areas of my life. It's pumped creativity into my other endeavors. It's strengthened many of my skill sets. It's given me confidence to branch out professionally in ways I didn't know were possible, and it's created opportunities in the form of other projects.

So much has come out of this small but mighty collaboration. It's shown me that the gift of a dream posture isn't some tangible product or achievement realized. The gift is the beauty of who we become. The gift is our eyes wide open to all that is already around us and within us. This gift changes us. It changes what we want and what we think we need. It changes how we move in the world.

We can be people who aren't afraid to dream up wildly good things for ourselves. We can dance with paradox, taking risks even as we hold our expectations and visions lightly. We can believe abundance is for us, knowing there is power in believing and there is power in us.

MANIFEST ABUNDANCE

So here is what we do. And I say this with my whole heart and zero triviality. I say it in light of every trauma under my belt and every ounce of grief I've known. Do we want to step into abundance? Well, then, we manifest it.

One fall evening, I was outside on my patio writing an op-ed piece. Suddenly, I had an epiphany and simultaneously a burst of excited energy. Around that same moment, my husband came outside, and I heard myself saying to him, "I'm manifesting good things for myself."

This was language I had never spoken or even thought before. It was as if Spirit rose up out of me and spoke those words. They caught me by such surprise that I laughed out loud after I said them. But I also held them close. I reflected on them, and I began paying deeper attention moving forward.

Here's what that patio epiphany revealed to me: just as we are the ones who must give ourselves permission to step into our healing journeys, and just as we are the only ones who can learn to trust our own intuition, *manifesting abundance in our lives requires our participation.*

Manifestation is not something that happens *to* us. It's not luck of the draw or a trick with the snap of our fingers. It is a process that we actually have some control over because it's an energy space that we can choose to enter into. What's more, manifestation can be looked at as a spiritual practice, because when cultivated, it helps us stay in alignment with our *imago Dei.*

I define manifestation as the act of creating new realities for ourselves by changing our usual responses. When in conflict, when triggered, when experiencing roadblocks, manifesting always involves a willingness to disrupt our own patterns.

Of course, it's easier said than done because when we disrupt our patterns, we will inevitably disrupt the systems around us as well. Families and other relationships will react to our decision to manifest something new in our lives. Sometimes this miraculously works just fine, but other times it can be painful. It can be tempting to turn back.

Regardless, we have permission to claim abundance if we want it. We have the ability to cultivate the patience and stamina needed to move past our fears and into a new way of seeing and being. Our authenticity and dreaming feed off of each another,

75

giving us access to clarity. And we've got wisdom from the Spirit in us granting us discernment. In other words, we have all we need *in abundance*. This includes the power to manifest.

ABUNDANCE TRANSFIGURES US

Abundance is both available to us and already accessible within us. When we tap into it, it will change us. But it won't just *change* us. Abundance *transfigures* us.

One of my favorite stories about Jesus is the one of the transfiguration, when Jesus leads his closest friends up to a mountaintop and reveals the fullness of his identity to them. I like to imagine that Jesus shone so bright that his dirty travel clothes looked pristine, and his face shone like the sun. I like to imagine his friends, jaws dropped to the ground, seeing Jesus in a new way, unrecognizable.

This is what transfiguration means. It means a complete change of form or appearance into a more beautiful or spiritual state. Abundance transfigures us in this way. Our selves that once acted out of scarcity, trauma, and pain become unrecognizable to us. The way we live and move transforms us because we've started doing things we've never done, such as believing deeper and fuller truths for ourselves.

So transfiguration is for us. Dreaming and manifesting are for us. Abundance is for us. And it isn't hokey. It's holy work. It's sacred posturing.

Listen: I am not giving you platitudes here. I am not saying that your struggle with mental health or your grief or your God-given personality makeup is going to suddenly transform, and everything is going to be A-OK. I'm not saying things will be *easy* or that there will be no need for community, professional help, or medicine. Not at all. Things will be complicated because life is hard, and we will need all the help we can get, and damn it, we should take it!

My belief in abundance has not come without its own cost. Like any good Spirit gift, it has certainly not come without work. I've had to dig deeper into my anxiety and into my traumas and hurts. I've had to dig deep into these shadow spaces and learn what it means to believe *anyway*. To have faith *anyway*. To love myself *anyway*.

And I love you too. Because you are me, and I am you. And I am climbing down into the depths with you in solidarity. I am searching for anything that could aid us in these times. I am determined to grab hold of any blessing that might usher us forward as we seek to live into the fullness of our birthright—our *imago Dei*.

If it's still difficult to believe in so much goodness, so much abundance swirling around us and within us, at least start here, with this small act of faith: You have more permission and power than you think.

8

Step into
PERMISSION

TRUST YOUR SPIRIT

One morning several years ago, I had an unexpected Divine encounter. My eyes had just opened, and I was in that dream-like in-between space where we haven't yet remembered and we haven't yet become. We haven't remembered the burdens of our life and we haven't become distracted by the demands of our day. Our minds are fertile. They are extra malleable to our subconscious and our deeper inner thoughts.

Groggy, I stumbled to the restroom as I willed myself to alertness. Suddenly, a panicked chain of thoughts hit me, one after another. It was like a domino effect: Boom! Boom! Boom!

What if you lose it all? Your family, your husband, your child,
everything you have? Everyone you love? Your comfort, your
security? What if you lost it? It could happen, you know. Then
what would you do?

At the same moment, I thought to myself worriedly, *How will I ever find peace and some semblance of certainty when it comes to my faith? If I so often feel confused and doubtful and unsure of everything now, how will I ever work out my beliefs in the worst of times?*

And this was the real problem, because the first set of questions I could throw off as irrational (and as an enneagram six, typical) once my mind was clear enough to reclaim my self-awareness. But the second set of questions triggered something inside me. They brought up remnants of a faith crisis that began in seminary and never really ended because real faith work involves deconstructing what you thought you believed from time to time. It's unavoidable. Authentic faith takes lots of work. It requires our care, our maintenance, and our energy every single (add expletive here!) day.

At that moment, I felt this reality hit me: After seminary, I had managed to piece together a version of a faith that worked but was only sustainable in the best of times. I realized this was unsteady ground I could not depend on. And so that morning moment was a reckoning as I came to terms with how little I could count on. All these panicked thoughts washed over me in moments—literally. I'm still on the toilet in this story! It all happened in seconds.

So I got up. I washed my hands, and I began readying myself to face the day. But the fear that swept over me in that moment was like a downpour. It broke something open in me. It was an undoing. I didn't want it. But then a voice spoke into the chaos of my soul. And the voice was stillness. It was calm. It was peace. It was God, but it was *inside* me. Without missing a beat, the voice said, "You will never have certainty about God if you don't trust your own Spirit."

God in me. *Imago Dei*, I thought.

Right there in that moment, jarred awake by this revelation, I embarked on the journey of listening to and trusting my own Spirit.

This may seem simple and possibly even anticlimactic. But for this brown woman, listening to my own Spirit and going with *that* despite what society or the church has told me has been a revelation worthy of daily reminder. You are worthy of this reminder too.

A BLESSING OF PERMISSION

So here's what I'm saying: *You* have the very Spirit of God within you, and it is God. Trust it. You have permission.

To the woman who has been told again and again in word, action, and lack of action to shut the hell up, to keep quiet, to stay small: Take up your space. Use your voice. Trust God in you.

To the queer person who has been swept off the path of faith community. Blackballed from the church. Cast out and ostracized. Questioned and rejected at the core of who you are. Forced to find other ways to God, often in isolation. You are a reflection of Divine image. Trust God in you.

To the person of color who has had to accept a white narrative of God. Who has muted yourself and code switched to no end. Whose ideas have been everything from belittled to stolen.

Your experience matters. Your existence is valuable. Trust God in you.

To the person unseen because of your disability, your documentation status, your financial struggle, your diagnosis. You are good. You are whole. Trust God in you.

And to the person of privilege, trust God in you. This is a blessing, yes. But it is also a challenge. We claim ownership of our *imago Dei, and* we acknowledge the full *imago Dei* in others rather than letting the systems we benefit from say otherwise. Much sacrifice and work are required in this. But it's important to remember we have this responsibility.

So go on. Do it! Trust God in you.

NO ONE BUT YOURSELF

For a long time, I didn't refer to myself as a woman of color. I had a whole reserve of racial traumas stored up because of the color of my skin, but because I didn't grow up in community with people who shared my background, I didn't think I had permission. It didn't help that my grandma would tease me, calling me a coconut. She'd say, "You're brown on the outside, white on the inside, and you can't speak Spanish!" Like clockwork, I would reply, "It's your fault I can't. You didn't teach your own kids your language!"

This was our bit. We'd say it with a laugh, tossing shame back and forth between each other like a Ping-Pong ball. And even though it was a joke between us, the words sunk in deep and settled within me.

I spent my childhood and young adulthood both disconnected from my brownness and relentlessly teased for it. When I
got wise enough to see the beauty of my roots, the shame set in.
I don't speak Spanish. I have no wider community. I don't belong.

When I moved to Texas in my adulthood, this shame deep-
ened. I felt disconnected to the people and the culture around
me, which brought up a lot of grief. I was too anxious to enter
Latine spaces. Every time I took Spanish classes, I was overwhelmed with emotion, making it difficult to engage in actual
learning.

Then one summer, I read Gloria Anzaldúa for the first time.
She was telling her story, but also the story of generational
trauma and liminality. And she was saying radically healing
things like "*I will no longer be made to feel ashamed of exist-
ing. I will have my voice: Indian, Spanish, white. I will have my
serpent's tongue—my woman's voice, my sexual voice, my poet's
voice. I will overcome the tradition of silence.*"[3]

Now I see my life in two parts: before I read Anzaldúa's work
and after I read it. In her book *Borderlands/La Frontera: The
New Mestiza,* I felt seen for the first time. Like I had come home
to myself. All I had experienced living in an in-between space
suddenly made sense, and I wasn't alone in those feelings. I was
more connected than I ever could have known. In her family's
story, I also saw my grandmother's lived experience. With a new
lens, I looked back with deeper knowing on encounters with
my grandma and her own shame. I realized that our healing is
wrapped up together.

Here is what I'm learning: No one can give you permission to step into healing but yourself. No one can give you permission to exist and to belong but yourself.

Once we find this inner permission and self-trust, we are compelled to move and speak from this powerful place. Inevitably, there is nothing we can do but take up our space. Anything else is a muted version of being.

PAY ATTENTION

Permission empowers us to reclaim what has always been true: God dwells within us. Spirit speaks *to us,* and we can trust this voice. But while permission is essential, it's meaningless without our undivided attention. It's not enough to trust our Spirit. We must learn to listen to it. We must become people who are paying attention.

The good news is we aren't starting from scratch. There is a voice that speaks to us daily already. The voice is our intuition, and this inner voice is trustworthy.

Think about it: We walk by a power cord and think to ourselves, *I should move that out of the way.* We don't, and we trip over it later. We see something we'll need as we are leaving our home and think, *I really ought to grab that now so I don't forget.* We don't. We forget it later.

We do the same with everything from our big-life choices to Spirit's movement within us. Our instinct is already there, speaking to us daily. It sends us messages, yet we don't often act on what it's telling us. Instead, we struggle to trust ourselves without layers and layers of outside permission.

But once we realize we don't need outside permission to hear our own Divine intuition speaking, the walls that once bound us can come tumbling down. At first, it might feel like a downpour, like something in us has broken open. But perhaps this undoing isn't so unwanted after all. Perhaps it is exactly what we need to step into alignment with our *imago Dei*. Operating from this alignment is to brush up against our God-given power.

So practice paying attention. Listen to your inner voice in whatever way makes sense to you. Practice honoring what you hear. Practice and then practice some more. Even as we function in community and walk alongside each other, we must consistently prioritize our own listening process.

Our own faith is not sustainable when it's tethered to the opinions of others. To one person we may be a heretic, and to another we'll never be woke enough. Regardless, at the end of the day we are responsible for our own faith foundation. The home within ourselves needs our loving attention.

YOUR HEART ISN'T DECEITFUL

When I was eleven years old, still reeling from the absence of my mother, I turned to God to cope with my pain and loneliness. At some point, I decided that I would read the whole Bible from beginning to end. It took me two years, but I did it. On my own— no adult guidance or permission required—I read every word. Every time a verse brought me comfort, I wrote it down on a slip of paper and put it into a shoebox that contained my favorite passages.

I found one particular text from the book of Jeremiah that was especially comforting when I was struggling. It said:

Blessed are those who trust in God,

whose trust is in God.

They shall be like a tree planted by water,

sending out its roots by the stream.

It shall not fear when heat comes,

and its leaves shall stay green;

in the year of drought it is not anxious,

and it does not cease to bear fruit.

(Jeremiah 17:7–8, New Revised Standard Version)

When I read these words, I felt like I could be strong and brave, despite all that had happened. I could know peace instead of pain. I could be free from fear and anxiety *if* I trusted in God, which I did. I placed all my trust in God because this was the formula. Sounds harmless, even helpful, right? But what came next in that text from Jeremiah would unfortunately shape me too. Verse 9 said:

The heart is devious above all else;

it is perverse—

Who can understand it?

(Jeremiah 17:9)

The heart is perverse. My heart. In my young, dualistic mind, I begin to believe deep down that God was good and I was bad.

So I spent my adolescence reeling from trauma and simultaneously drilling into my head that my own heart couldn't be trusted. That I couldn't trust myself. And that if I felt something in my gut, it was probably wrong.

For years, I thought that operating this way was the definition of humility. But now I understand that what I was doing was diminishing my own God-given Spirit. And the truth is I wasn't the only kid ingesting this harmful interpretation around this exact text. Christian leaders have long used this verse to manipulate, indoctrinate, and control. Intentional or not, the impact is the same.

We become people who do not trust ourselves. We second-guess the way we navigate life and the way we make decisions. In our efforts to be good and faithful, we become people with *less* faith because we keep waiting for permission from someone else. Permission to believe that God truly dwells within us. And yet this permission was always ours, and it's not too late to reclaim it.

If our hope is Divine intimacy, believing our hearts are deceitful actually separates us from God. It creates a rift between us and God by making us suspicious of our own selves, the very place where the Spirit of God dwells. The more we learn to trust Spirit in us, the easier it becomes to reject nonsense paradigms like this one, even as they are continually perpetuated by Christian culture.

Stepping into permission involves reclaiming what bad theology took away from us. We can do things differently. We are allowed. We can trust our intuition, our creativity, our ideas, and our abilities. We can do radical things like trust our own voice and then use it. We can do wild things such as choose to belong to ourselves. We can even do this: we can love ourselves a whole damn lot. It's absolutely possible.

9

Step into
YOUR CHILD SELF

THE EGG

My mom-in-law, Melinda, is an artist, a healer, and the owner
of the Ophelia Center, which houses a Harmonic Egg here in
Austin, Texas. The Harmonic Egg is a chamber that uses sacred
geometry, light, color, and sound frequencies to empower your
body's healing energy.

My first time in the Egg was brief yet intense. We were cel-
ebrating Melinda's business opening with a family dinner. Even
though it's usually an hour-long experience, each of us took
fifteen minutes to try it out. When it was my turn, Melinda led
me to a quiet room with relaxing energy and low light. Once in
the room, she invited me to step into the chamber, which had a
reclining chair. After helping me get settled in with loving intention, she began to close me in.

As Melinda shut the door to the chamber, I could hear my young daughter, who had followed us down the hallway, crying out, "I want Mommy!" Though I was now alone, surrounded only by the sights and sounds of the Harmonic Egg, I could hear Melinda scooping her up and shutting the door to the room. And I could still hear the soft cries of "I want Mommy! I want Mommy!" as they headed up the hallway to join the rest of our family.

I was not prepared for what came next. I experienced an embodied trauma response. My head became so heavy it was hard to lift it, and I could barely open my mouth. My senses were in overdrive as I took in the calming energy of the Egg while simultaneously hearing the muffled cries of my daughter. I was triggered.

Suddenly, I was brought back to another time and place: I was twelve years old, back in rural north Louisiana in that little house on Bolling Drive. It was late at night, so my dad was asleep, and my sister had just left home to join the military. I was hunched into a corner of the cold bathroom floor, sobbing into my knees and crying out for my mother in between breaths. "I want you, Mom!" I said over and over again.

I felt utterly alone in the world. Panicked by the depth of loneliness I was experiencing. My little mind was in overdrive trying to comprehend all my big feelings and fears. I thought I'd forgotten this memory until my body reminded me otherwise. All this passed through me within minutes, and I found myself frantically wiping away tears and taking deep breaths, desperately trying to pull myself out of the memory before my brief time in the Egg ran out.

When Melinda opened the chamber to help me out, something in me had shifted. I was able to engage and even enjoy the rest of the evening, but once I got home, I went straight to my office. I needed to write down what happened so I could try to make sense of it.

I realized that while my experience was overwhelming, that short time showed me something of great value. It brought my attention back to my child self. It was a reunion between me and little Aurelia. I am thankful for this moment of clarity that helped me see not only some ways my child self still needs healing but also the many gifts she still seeks to offer me.

SACRED REMEMBERING

Tending to your child self is both healing work and spiritual practice at once. It is the liberation of little you. Little you is wounded. Little you is also bursting with potential. Little you needs love and care, and at the same time, little you has resources to offer in the present moment.

Little you extends an ongoing invitation to come back to yourself. Come back to *you* before your creativity and wonder were stripped from you. Before the harsh realities of life had their say. Before the indoctrination set in. After so many years of disconnect, behold little you with grace and gratitude. This is your *imago Dei* in its purest form.

Coming back requires *looking* back, which is not the same as *going* back. Rather, this work is uncovering. The work is acknowledgment. It is a spiritual and an emotional excavation. We dig up some things, and we hold what we discover to the light in its entirety. This is our do-over. Our opportunity to treat ourselves with the self-compassion we couldn't garner back then.

Would we ever be intentionally unkind to a suffering child? The answer is no. There's no need to be unkind to the child within us either. We can offer little us loving kindness through the act of this sacred remembering. We do this so that the story we embody in the future can finally move beyond our trauma. The end goal is that our decisions, our interactions, and the rhythm of our lives are informed by *imago Dei*, as opposed to what should have or shouldn't have happened to us.

As you remember, ask yourself: what does your child self need to hear *now*? What does your child self need to feel loved *now*?

When I was in that Harmonic Egg and that unexpected memory skyrocketed to the surface of my mind, I knew it was only the fringes of the trauma I had buried. I didn't do it consciously, of course. But as I began to wake up and step into my fullness, every part of me began to wake up too. Not just the powerful parts of me, but the hidden and hurting parts as well. I couldn't pick and choose. I didn't want to anymore.

THIS IS PAINFUL

Can you think about your child self without emotion? Can you go into an uninterrupted space of reflecting on little you without a level of empathy rising up and out? It's entirely easy to be critical of our present selves, but our hearts will ease up when it comes to little us.

It's less difficult for us to look upon our child selves with patience and understanding than it is to do the same for us as adults. But this doesn't mean it's not painful. Because when we come face-to-face with our young self, we come face-to-face with the most vulnerable parts of us. The traumas and triggers and work involved may be distinct to each individual, but there is not one of us immune to the need of this work.

We must prioritize caring for the child still dwelling within us. We must reclaim the voice of that child as well. In my own painful solidarity, I invite you into this work. Because our fullness requires the healing of all of ourselves.

IT'S NOT TOO LATE

We are living in unprecedented times. A global pandemic has connected us to suffering in a unique way. We are positioned for a collective uncovering as well. Some people are finally waking up. Others are finally speaking their truth. On so many levels, we are experiencing upheaval as old, harmful systems die.

From this place, we have an opportunity to create new ways of being in the world, free from hierarchical systems and limitations. I suppose this should be a hopeful sentiment, and yet if you are like me, perhaps you struggle being hopeful at all. Maybe you can agree with me that there is a lot about living on planet Earth that looks bleak right now. As a parent, it can be scary raising kids in times like these.

But when I look to the future through the eyes of my daughter, I see an alternate reality. And it is for her sake that I am motivated to create the kind of world she believes is possible.

The kind of world she assumes is inevitable. I'm willing to entertain imagining the world the way she does and I'm energized to create this alternate reality for her sake, for mine, and for all of us.

If you were to dig deep and really behold your child self, I wonder if you wouldn't be motivated to do some radical imagining as well. Because when you look at that little child who still lives inside you, you know they deserve more than the reality they lived. And you want more for them now too. I'm saying that it's not too late.

WE AREN'T JUST TRAUMATIZED; WE ARE ALSO RESOURCED

My kid is like every other kid on the planet in that she's not all that jazzed about vegetables. I mean, sure, she has her favorites. But if she has to choose between a snap pea and a popsicle, she's headed to the freezer every single time. I'm constantly telling her why vegetables are valuable. How she needs them to grow healthy and strong. And she is a child, which means she's a sponge too.

She's also an almost kindergartner. In fact, I'm currently grieving the last few weeks I have at home with her before school starts. No baby here. She is 100 percent an official kid. The other day, I asked her jokingly, "Why do you keep growing?" Totally serious, she responded, "Mom, I can't help it. Healthy people grow."

Indeed they do, my girl. Healthy people grow. And that's what we do too. We grow. We move. We shift, evolve, expand.

We move forward, and yet there are also moments of moving back (we are paradox people, remember?).

We step into our child self, not just because we are traumatized people who need healing but because we are resourced people who deserve abundance. And our child self has unlimited gifts to offer us if we are brave enough to pay attention.

Only you can decide to take this particular journey. Along the way, you will likely discover a need for help. We weren't meant to go it alone. You may need therapy or medication or both. You might need to prioritize some relationships and let others go. You may need to create new rhythms and boundaries in your life. Only you are the expert of your own healing.

For those interested in what Jesus had to say about it, this alternate reality that seems so hopeless or naïve to us is actually not so far off. Jesus said that the child's instinct and the childlike posture are the closest vision we have of fathoming the kin-dom of heaven.[4]

And this instinct Jesus talked about, we still have it. It may be buried deep, but it lives within each one of us and always has. Our child self, the purest form of our *imago Dei*, never left us. We can be our own healing catalyst. We are overflowing with gifts to make it happen.

A NONEXHAUSTIVE LIST OF CHILD-SELF GIFTS

Growth: Spirit-movement in our lives is a given, but we are now able to recognize it. We listen, learn, observe, ask questions. We prioritize curiosity. We put good things into our bodies, we nurture our energy, and we protect our headspace. We become people who are just always growing.

Resilience: We know from our own experience—for better or worse—that children are resilient. Children endure so much, and still they grow: they laugh, they play, they become. We still have access to this kind of resilience. We can do hard things, we can survive despite what has hurt us, we can heal, and we can experience profound joy and hope and love.

Acceptance: We can accept our realities even as Spirit compels us toward more. We can accept others as they are even as we work toward collective liberation. We can step outside of either/or, binary thinking, and into something much more imaginative. Something more reflective of the alternate realities we have the capacity to envision.

Creativity: We use creativity and imagination to engage the Divine, practice gratitude, and look ahead to our work. We can use our brains to solve tough problems; we can innovate and trailblaze. We can use these tools to build the realities we want to see. We don't have to wait. We are ready to build.

Play: This one is my favorite and is so important. We simply need play. We need fun; we need celebration and joy, even now. And we need it to be instinctual and readily accessible. This is play that is deeper than our circumstances. Not meant to be a quick fix but simply a part of who we are and how we exist in the world no matter what we are facing.

These tools are nothing more than the markers of a child: growth, resilience, acceptance, creativity, play. It's a nonexhaustive list that is available to us right now. But we won't gain access to the fullness of these gifts without engaging the areas of healing within us. This means we face the realities of our traumas. We go deep within ourselves to that place where our child still lives and calls out to us. With Divine help, we can tend to that dear child's wounds.

10

Step into
GOODNESS

REDEFINING GREATNESS

I am one of those unfortunate souls who suffer regularly from
FOMO (otherwise known as the *fear of missing out*). I hate
feeling left out, and it's likely because I often *was* left out in
childhood. I know I wasn't the only kid who felt overlooked or
underestimated at some point. For me, it was witnessing this
kind of behavior from adults in my community that left the
biggest imprint.

Growing up, I observed my mom being purposely left out
of community by women in our church time and time again. I
experienced it myself as early as elementary school, where the
white kids were regularly preferenced for special invitations in
the arts or in school programming. I even remember when the
parents of my sister's white boyfriend went to great lengths to
get their son to stop dating her. This included telling him she

had a secret boyfriend in Mexico, a country she had never even visited.

In my family, we've only recently begun voicing our stories with a shared knowing. Back then, we never talked in real time about what it felt like to exist in small-town Louisiana. Instead, we each coped with our realities in isolation. Still, while we didn't often speak of the toll these circumstances took on us individually, we always had each other's backs in practice. I especially felt this support as the youngest in my family.

I had older sisters who mothered me every chance they could, including financially. From paying for my junior-high cheer fees, to my first laptop in college, and then to my wedding dress, my sisters made every effort to make my life easier than theirs had been. I also had a father who was supportive and involved. He bent over backward to see to my happiness and provision (and still does). My sisters and dad surrounded me with opportunities that would ensure my good health and thriving. This energized me to harness my ambition and then use it to my advantage.

So even if it meant saving my tears for when I got home at the end of the day, I did what Kamala Harris said, and "I ate no for breakfast." Indeed, outside of my home, it felt like one big "NO" had been placed over my life without my say in it. And my response was to become not just good but *great*. I sought greatness out through a veil of perfection: perfect grades, perfect rule-following, perfect Christian. I learned how to read a room and be a chameleon, becoming what I needed to be in any given context. In this way, I became a compulsive people pleaser and overachiever.

I'll be the first to tell you there's nothing wrong with ambition. Mine has served me well, and I have no intention of rejecting this part of myself. The problem is that I became someone whose existence was a reaction. My pursuit of greatness was a *response* to never feeling like I was enough, and I didn't know myself outside of it. This defensive posture is not the place for greatness to be born.

Rewriting our narrative, reclaiming our intuition, and stepping into our power each involve redefining what it means to be great. Greatness and goodness are not in competition with each other. Both are rooted in the power of our *imago Dei*. But greatness rooted in ego, in hierarchy, and in productivity culture is not what's best for us. Instead, we step into our *goodness* as our way forward, understanding that this is the pathway to true greatness.

WE WERE MADE GOOD

I was preparing for a small dinner party, when I asked my daughter if she'd help me set the table. She loves whenever we use our placemats and cloth napkins, so I knew she'd be delighted. As we laid everything out together, her eyes beamed with pride, and she said to me, "*I'm helping you because I want to be a good girl.*"

Damn it if this didn't trigger me! Because I know full well that I still find myself trying to earn my goodness. I'm constantly doing and doing and doing. And hoping that by all my doing, I will be "good." This is no way to live. So I told my daughter the truth in hopes that she won't have to reclaim it later. Perhaps she could always be connected to her fullness.

I said, *"Thank you for helping me. It is very kind, and it makes me feel loved. But you do not have to help me to be a good girl. You are already good whether you help me or not. God created you good."*

I said this even as I struggle to embody it myself because I truly believe we can come to believe that our goodness is unconditional. We can undo the wiring that has told us otherwise. Our goodness is not defined by what we do. We were made *good.*

BAD THEOLOGY STRIKES AGAIN

There is a reason people often think they have to earn their goodness, and it goes back to bad theology designed to scare us into submission. There's even a fancy theological name for it. It's called *original sin*, and it's religious jargon suggesting that we were born tainted, with a natural proclivity to be sinful.

I used to read other theologians for all of my permission, but now I know the truth of it. Which is that I'm a bona fide theologian myself. I've got years of biblical study under my belt, a whole-ass seminary education, and more than a decade of pastoral work in my current church setting. So with every bit of "authority" I can muster, I'm telling you right now: original sin is actual utter bullshit.

And yet this framework has seeped down through our tradition over time, informing our cultures, our language, and our societal norms. Even if you aren't remotely religious, this concept has been given power over many of our lives and belief systems.

Why do you think it's difficult for many of us to stop and rest? Or to say no or set healthy boundaries? Why are we so driven by guilt and shame? Because we are people who are addicted to earning our goodness and worthiness. It has been drilled into us from childhood that this is the way.

Yet the heartbeat of *imago Dei* is this: we are made in God's image. God dwells within us. We are made up of the stuff of love. We are good. We are good. We are good! So it follows that we find healing in this goodness. It is Divine goodness that is already available to us because it is quite literally our birthright. God in us.

BELIEVING OUR GOODNESS

The problem is we've got it out of order. We want to *do* good so that eventually we might come to believe we *are* good. But what happens if we just decide to believe we are good, right here, right now, no strings attached?

Here's what happens: everything changes.

Let's make the shift. Let's choose to believe we are already good instead of trying to earn our way to goodness. But what does it mean to be good?

For many of us, our faith teaches that God is love and God is good. If we are made in God's image and God's Spirit lives in us, then we are made up of this same love and goodness. It really is this simple. But people and systems have wanted to complicate this basic truth.

For some of us, goodness has meant not rocking the boat. Stay bent, stay small. For some, to be good has meant to be successful, to thrive at all costs. For others, goodness has looked like holy checklists (am I being good enough for God or others?). Regardless, what all of these definitions of goodness have in common is that at some point, we *will* inevitably fall short.

This is why it's so important to *believe* we are good first and foremost instead of tying our goodness to impossible conditions. Believing *first* enables us to access self-compassion, which is a must-have on this journey. It also expands our capacity for grace and deepens our faith. When we believe first, we become equipped to identify what goodness is and what it is not. We re-lay our foundation.

WHAT GOODNESS IS NOT

There are a lot of unnecessary belief systems we need to question and let go of, but here's a good place to start: Our goodness is not about our personal piety. In fact, personal piety is of little value to us at all. It is a people-pleasing cover. It is spirituality with ego in tow. More often than not, it gets in our way. Because Spirit practice sans ego is the authentic faith posture we seek, shifting our consciousness here can only benefit us.

Here's another: Our goodness is not tied to purity culture. Men, women, and every gender in between and beyond need to hear this one. We've already begun to notice the harm perpetuated by purity culture, including toxic masculinity and violence against women and queer folks. Purity culture, rooted in bad theology and lazy interpretations of Scripture, causes suffering for all of us.

Jesus had a thing or two to say about purity, but it had nothing to do with pious acts, how we dress, our gender identity, or who we have sex with. Instead, Jesus tied purity to goodness when he said, "Blessed are the pure in heart, for they will see God" (Matthew 5:8). This *imago Dei*-informed nugget of truth is sandwiched between the rest of his pinnacle teaching of the Beatitudes.

Here, Jesus redefines greatness, shifting the focus to goodness and then turning the definition of goodness on its head. Goodness is not having power over others. It's not about reputation or status. Goodness is about extending peace. It is about showing mercy. It is vulnerability embodied. And it operates outside of the status quo, which means it is inherently disruptive.

Stepping into this goodness will disrupt your life, insisting that you step into a more meaningful existence (and not taking *no* for an answer). And it will disrupt those around you. Those who may not yet understand your commitment to this counter-cultural goodness will react in their own ways.

Regardless, you step in because you are no longer bound to outside authority. Not on your spiritual journey. Not with your healing work. And certainly not when it comes to something as vital as believing in the truth of your utter goodness.

GOODNESS FOUND ON THE MARGINS

Each of us has a different relationship to the Bible. Maybe you've never read it, or maybe you never want to read it again (trust me, I get it). In either case, let me offer my own summary of this complex collection of books: The Bible is a sacred text in which the Divine elevates the poor, the oppressed, the immigrants, the women, and others despite all societal odds being against them. From the first books of the Torah, to the life of Christ, to the story of Paul, God has a preferential option for the poor and those most vulnerable.

If you are looking for something shorter, here's an alternate summary of the Bible: in which God's inclusive agenda shines through the muck of patriarchy. In either summary, the same fundamental truth shines through: our alignment with the Divine is best found on the margins of society.

Jesus lived, moved, and ministered from the margins. His way was antithetical to that of empire and even his own religious leaders. He was not a model religious person, because he questioned most things and disregarded the rest. He didn't throw everything out, but he looked through a radically new lens: a concern for goodness over greatness.

The way Jesus did this was by taking his cues from the margins every single time. Imagine if we did the same. Imagine if we looked to the most oppressed, neglected, and vulnerable in and around our society. The poor. The children and elderly. The immigrants. Black people, Indigenous people, and people of color. Those disabled. Women. The LGBTQIA community. What if we believed their stories and gave ear to their wisdom? What if we honored their needs? What if *this* was the spiritual practice of goodness?

I am of the opinion that this is what it means to sit at the feet of Jesus in our day. Which is why I am compelled to continue in the practice of following the Christ path. Divine alignment is sitting at the feet of the very people whose *imago Dei* has been most neglected. Not by changing them. Not by saving them. By sitting at their feet with a posture of humility and love.

We see the face of God here, and so goodness will certainly be found here as well. If we can find goodness, we can believe it. If we can believe it, we can finally begin to embody it.

MAY WE LAY DOWN OUR DEFENSES

In truth, goodness is so much more difficult than greatness. Greatness is the easy way out. It is all ego, which is all surface. Goodness asks more of us. It requires reckless abandon of our ego-defenses.

After my daughter was born, I noticed that she always had her fists curled up when she was sleeping. She was so tense every time she slept. And if anyone touched her or she heard a noise, in her sleep, she would clench her little fists even tighter and bring them to her face as if to protect herself.

Many of us are moving through our lives with our fists up, defensive and wary. And who could blame us? We have been burned and betrayed time and again. On top of that, everything that is required of us is uncomfortable. As a collective, we continue to struggle to lay down our guard. We are pushing and pulling under the weight of old paradigms, and we are tired.

If you resonate with this, you are right where you should be. Welcome to life. This leaning in and letting go over and over again is the work of goodness, and you are doing it! You are trusting God in you by not being afraid to take your own journey. And you are not looking away from the collective connection. You are beginning to understand your place in the Oneness of all things. You are learning how to live in the beauty of paradox. This is good. And so are you.

II

Step into
THE DIVINE FEMININE

Divine Mother,
why do you scare me,
why can't I break free
still?

Divine Mother,
what keeps me from you,
which trauma is it?

Is it the patriarchal wound
so deep, so painful,
sending all the same messages
still?

Or is it the betrayal of my mother,
is your face too similar to her face,
is that why it hurts to draw near
sometimes?

Divine Mother,
what keeps me from you,
which trauma is it?

GOD IN HER FULLNESS

Years ago, I spent a few days at a Benedictine monastery just outside of Portland, in Mt. Angel, Oregon. One day while exploring a wooded area, I found a path leading inward. With the tall Oregon trees both shading and concealing me, the trail led me to a bench facing a statue of the Virgin Mary. I plopped down on the bench, and for a long time, I did nothing but stare at that statue.

I remembered a card I was given as a little girl that depicted the Virgin Mary. She was robed in blue, holding the Christ child in her arms. I still remember the first lines of the poem printed on the back. They read: "Lovely Lady dressed in blue; teach me how to pray. God was just your little boy, tell me what to say."

I loved that tiny card, and I carried it with me everywhere. Not only did it light me up inside to imagine Jesus as a child, but I also loved the image of Mary. I loved the Divine feminine imagery she represented. I loved that my mother shared her name. I loved how I felt close to God when I was close to her.

Indeed, for as long as I can remember, I knew God, and God knew me. That truth was as easy as breathing, and Mary was an important part of that story. But as I grew up in heavily Protestant north Louisiana, I was told by peers, adults, and religious leaders that Catholics worship Mary. I was told that even though I believed in God, loved Jesus, and prayed as a child better than I ever do now, my beliefs were wrong.

And you know what? I believed it. I began to lose touch with this faith of my childhood until it was only a distant memory. For years, I rejected anything tied to that version of faith in favor of the heavy-handed prescriptions of evangelicalism. Intuition, imagination, and any sense of freedom—I went to sleep to it all.

But something happened on that bench, in those woods, as I gazed upon the outreached arms of Mother Mary. I mourned what had been lost, but at the same time, something in me was reawakened. In that moment, I made a promise to myself. I vowed to reclaim every bit of freedom I had set aside.

I finally rose and retreated from my secret spot in the forest, but this time, I took a different path, the one leading to the reclamation of my fullness. And now I know it's true: if we want to step into our fullness, we must allow God to exist in her fullness too.

MOTHER-GOD HOPE

Mother's Day has long been a difficult holiday for me to acknowledge. Along with the countless women who have experienced pain or loss around motherhood or being mothers, I have experienced many Mother's Days filled with grief and loneliness.

It never helped that churches have long used this day to honor a mother's role in the family unit.

In fact, I have often wondered why we even talk about Mother's Day at church in the first place. What about it makes it theologically relevant? Perhaps it is because we understand and experience God through family metaphors. We've known God in the Christian faith predominantly as Father. We even know God as babe in the manger every year at Christmas. Maybe we throw so much emphasis, celebration, and reverence behind Mother's Day because we are subconsciously aware of how much Mother-God is missing from our faith equation.

I've got lots of gratitude for moms. I am one myself, and let's get real: it's a pretty thankless job a lot of the time. So I enjoy the extra attention my family gives me on Mother's Day. But everything that is true and wonderful about mothers is something we first see and learn from the Divine feminine. Mother-God.

The nature of mothering comes from God, and it is a part of each of us too. Woman, man, somewhere along the gender binary or beyond: each of us experiences mothering, and each of us practices mothering all the time because God defines mothering work. And God defines the nurturing love and energy we attribute to the concept of mother.

This is what God does for us: God mothers us by bringing us into new life. God mothers us by nourishing us with Divine presence. God mothers us, offering sustenance through Divine feminine hope. Mother-God wants us to be healed. She wants us—her children—to be well, to be healthy, to be protected and nurtured, and to know her unconditional love. The kind of love a mother gives.

Several years ago, I helped organize an interfaith retreat in our area. People and teachers from various faith communities met together for the day and taught each other practices from their faith tradition. The woman who spoke to us about Hinduism spoke about God and devotion in a way I'll never forget.

She compared our yearning for the Divine to a baby, specifically to an infant crying out for her mother. The baby doesn't know the mother's name, whether she's her biological mom or married, straight, or gay. She doesn't know if she's rich or poor, or if she's employed or educated. The baby doesn't know any of this. She only knows to cry out when she's tired, hungry, afraid, frustrated. The baby knows instinctively to cry out, and this mothering presence will come.

We do this too. We cry out to a God we don't completely know or understand, and yet on some level we know that this presence will show up. Somehow, in some way, we continue to believe in this presence. This is what it means to practice faith. Because we practice and never arrive, it's always work. It's always a challenge. Learning to live in the tension of it is the daily embodiment of surrender.

So we surrender. Moment by moment, we hold on to the hope of God. We do this hard thing because we hunger for Divine presence—a mothering presence. Ultimately, we want to know that we are safe, held, doted on, and provided for. We want to know Divine connection in this instinctual, mystical way.

We are *already* searching for Mother-God. Acknowledging this with shifts in our language and imagery helps tear down the walls that have been built up around her.

GOD AS SHE

In my experience being a pastor, nothing—*nothing*—gets people more riled up than speaking of God in the feminine. This is exactly why we need to normalize interchanging our pronouns of the Divine every chance we get. When we limit our understanding of God to one gender, we also limit the well of our own healing and hope because we limit the image of God within us.

This is why it's not enough to simply take away male pronouns for God. Taking away is a scarcity mindset, and we are living in abundance, where our understanding of God has broken wide open. From this place, *every* pronoun is up for grabs because we know we are tapping only the surface of Divine image. And yet we cannot get to this place without first becoming comfortable with *God as she.*

In her book *Thy Queendom Come: Breaking Free from the Patriarchy to Save Your Soul,* Kyndall Rae Rothaus says, "*I do not think we can balance the theological scales by adding a drop or two of nonbinary language about God.*"[5] I couldn't agree more for countless reasons, but here are two of the most obvious ones:

First, gender has been assigned to God, whether we like it or not. Over the course of Christian history, God has been assigned to the male gender based on the construct of patriarchy. But here's the problem: Patriarchal religion has put a Divine stamp on war and colonialism. Patriarchal theology tells some men that it's their God-given right to be violent toward women. Patriarchal values are why women in our country still struggle to enter the workforce and, once they do, are paid significantly less than men. Patriarchy is rooted in domination, and Christian theology continues to be informed and influenced by its harms.

Here's the other reason it's urgent we expand our image of God: we simply must bring the Divine down to earth so that we can intimately engage with God in a way that we can understand. Why do you think Christ needed to exist as a human person walking the earth? Similarly, if we are going to experience God or, at the very least, fathom God, we need metaphors. We need language, and we need to see ourselves in God and God in us. Every last one of us needs this kind of connection.

THIS ISN'T WOMEN'S TALK

The sexual violence, abuse, and harassment of women and girls is unparalleled. According to RAINN (Rape, Abuse & Incest National Network), the nation's largest antisexual violence organization, one in nine girls is a victim of sexual assault by adults, compared to one in fifty-three boys. Women have been viewed and treated as literal property over the course of centuries, and the effects of this are still in motion.

Because our personal healing is tied up in collective healing, this is relevant to all of us. We have to intervene. We have to alter the course of history. Part of this work requires admitting that there is real damage done to all of us when the things of God are limited to *he* and *him*.

What does it feel like for only masculine imagery of God to be used for a whole lifetime? For me, it feels like I am being kept from ever knowing and experiencing God fully. It feels like I am being prevented from recognizing the Spirit of God in me: my feminine self, my body, my heart.

If our little girls grow up hearing only *him* and *he* and *Father* when it comes to the image of God, where is their sense of *imago Dei*? If little boys grow up hearing only *him* and *he* and *Father* when it comes to the image of God, how will they ever learn to value girls and women in a way that is wholly reflective of Jesus? And what about our gender nonconforming kids who are facing bullying, abuse, and violence because of their gender fluidity?

So, there are a lot of reasons women specifically need this liberating word. We've been wounded, and we carry this feminine wound in us in a unique way. But this isn't "women's talk."

So many of us are missing out on the fullness of God. We know parts of God, we have bits of faith, but the fullness of God has not been ours yet. Which means we are also missing out on the fullness of ourselves because our *imago Dei* is based on *all* of the Divine, the whole picture, not just a part of it. With great urgency, may we develop an expanded consciousness of the image of God. For the sake of all our children and their *imago Dei*, may we begin embodying this expanded consciousness via our own language.

SACRED SNAKES

In the spring of 2020, the world had all but shut down due to COVID-19. Almost everything was closed. Almost everyone was home. The world was slow and quiet, and we were all uncertain. And during this time, I had an unexpected season of encountering snakes.

As with a lot of people, my rhythm of life had abruptly changed, and I found myself tending to projects around my house. It had been my goal going into 2020 to begin worm composting, and now that I was home literally all the time, I had some space to make this happen.

One afternoon, I decided to measure the space in my yard where I was considering setting up the composting. The space I'd settled on used to be a garden, so even though grass had taken over the soil, the circumference of the space was still surrounded by a small barrier of rocks.

I stepped out the back door of my garage, preparing my heart and mind to do something spiritual—something that cared for the earth and would be a grounding practice for me. I walked down the stone steps that led to my yard, strolled toward the rock boundary, and when I went to step up and over that small wall, I almost stepped onto a snake that was at least four feet long! Startled, I ran inside. I found out later it was nonvenomous when my husband (aka, saint) went out and used a rake to scoop the snake up and toss it over our fence onto the other side of the greenbelt.

A week later, I decided I would take a meditative walk on a trail behind our house. I was preparing for a sermon and wanted to do some thinking and reflecting. To get onto the trail from where I live, you have to walk down the street, between two houses, and then step up and over a small fencelike barrier that lines the hill. I had walked down and lifted my leg to step onto the wall, when I nearly stopped on a large black snake. I jumped and ran all the way home. Ha! I was shocked and irritated that I had just seen two snakes in the span of a week.

I live in central Texas, and snakes are not uncommon. But I had lived in our home for three years at that point, and I had never seen a snake myself, not even once. The snake encounters continued. One day, I was walking up toward our back patio with my daughter. When I went to step up onto the patio step, there was a snake. Another time, I had just grabbed a notebook and a pencil with the intention of doing some writing on my back porch. When I looked up, right there on the patio, staring at me, was yet another snake. I even dreamed about snakes.

During this time, I was also working on a sermon about the Divine feminine. One day, I pulled out a beloved book, *The Dance of the Dissident Daughter,* by Sue Monk Kidd. I flipped through, looking at various parts I had underlined several years back. And I got to this part where she talks about the creation story and the snake's meaning in antiquity. She talks about how in ancient times, the snake was not feared but revered. It was a symbol of sacred feminine energy and power.

Immediately, I had chills go up and down my body. This thought reverberated through me: *What if those snakes were blessing the ground I was walking on?*

Does it sound like crazy talk to you? Maybe. Maybe not. The point is this: Something that scared me ended up a blessing— and not just a blessing but a *welcome.* Something that terrified me became an entry point to God.

We ought to do something similar when it comes to the Divine feminine. We need to explore why it scares us or repels us. Instead of retreating at the first moment of discomfort, we need to go as close as we can get.

Naming is a part of our collective beholding. Beholding is our inner work. We need to behold the Divine feminine. We need to lean in so that we can know the healing she has in store for us. We need to lean in so we can learn all she has to teach us, so we can cultivate the kind of hope she has to offer us.

We do all of this so we can live from deep within ourselves— and from this deep well know not just part but the fullness of God.

12

Step into
MYSTERY

MYSTERY IS HOLY GROUND

I'm writing as the COVID-19 delta variant ramps up in Texas. Plus, in a matter of days, I'll send my little girl off to kindergarten. With this season has come a whole lineup of difficult choices, all of which lead to some level of grief or emotional upheaval. Everything feels scary and uncertain. Everything seems to be lose/lose. In other words, reader, I'm writing this chapter as a whole hot mess.

Luckily, I recently picked up a copy of Pádraig Ó Tuama's book *In the Shelter: Finding a Home in the World*. Another way of saying this is a life preserver has been extended to me, just as I'm starting to go under. In a beautiful imagining of the disciples on the stormy sea being met by Jesus, Tuama observes, *"It is as if to say that only in the middle of a storm can we find a truth that will steady us."*[6]

Sigh. Perhaps I can do this hard thing of greeting the present just as I am and just as it is. Instead of retreating or resisting, maybe I could move deeper into *now*. Maybe I am capable of facing this particular moment in time.

When I face it, I realize I have been here before. And I am reminded of what a life of faith has shown me and what a global pandemic continues to reveal: that multiple things can be true at once. That sorrow and hopelessness and joy can all somehow coexist. And that this complicated, nuanced space is the birthplace of mystery. And mystery is exactly where we ought to be. Blessed are those who have the courage to enter in.

Blessed are the paradox people,
the nuance seekers,
the curious.

Blessed are the lifelong learners,
who greet failure with a kiss,
who practice and never arrive.

Blessed are the givers and receivers of sacred space,
who keep subtlety in tow,
which is to say

Blessed are those wise enough to see
that stepping into mystery
is to walk on holy ground.

Courage.
Today and every day.
Courage.

MYSTERY GIVES US PERMISSION TO WRESTLE

When I was a little girl, I believed in Jesus something fierce. He was just so real to me. I would draw pictures for him and tell my mom, *"This is for Jesus!"* I would read my Precious Moments Bible storybook over and over again, and I would lie in bed at night and just talk to him. I had no doubt he was present with me in those moments.

I was sure the only reason he didn't *visibly* show up was because he knew how much a ghostlike appearance would frighten me. So Jesus stayed invisible, but I could see him clearly through the stories I was taught. My favorites were those that spoke of him as a little boy. I loved Christmas because for once we would focus on Jesus as a child. I loved imagining him young, just like me. I loved him, and my faith in him was unmovable.

Fast forward a couple of decades to my first semester in seminary. I was lying on the bed of our new apartment in a new state, crying my eyes out. Everything I thought I knew had come undone. Every ounce of certainty I thought I had was gone. I was beginning to see how my mystical childhood relationship with Jesus had shifted over the years into a focus on manmade Christian dogma. Instead of believing in a Jesus so real I had to ask him not to appear to me, my faith felt flimsy, as one belief after another came tumbling down in academia.

In a matter of months, it seemed like my spiritual landscape had gone from rich soil, to windblown chaos, to desert place. I wondered, if one belief was thrown out, what did that mean for the next one in the queue? What did I believe at all anymore? Why was I getting this stupid degree to begin with? My faith was a domino effect disaster, and I was in full-blown panic mode.

I remember my husband sitting on the edge of our bed, trying to offer words of comfort by reminding me that my faith was a faith in *God*. Not the Bible. Not in theological frameworks. Not in any religious checklist. In his own way, he reminded me of my faith roots, and even if I couldn't see what lay ahead, what he told me was just enough. It was enough to help me dry my tears and finish my homework. To get into bed and get some sleep. To wake up the next day and put one foot in front of the other. I could do it. Inch by inch, I could make a tiny bit of room for the mystery of faith.

I wish I could say there was some moment where everything clicked and my faith crisis totally evaporated. But it took years for me to finally realize that this is simply what it looks like. This is what it means to do my own faith work. Namely, it is a commitment to daily wrestling.

Many of us grew up in contexts that told us it was wrong to doubt or ask questions about the things of God. If we wrestled, we did it in shame-filled privacy. But when we can embrace mystery, we realize that wrestling is the secret ingredient to a sustainable and thriving faith journey.

So we wrestle. We wrestle as a lifelong art of faith practice. We wrestle because we have been liberated from certainty. We wrestle because we are holding many truths at once. We wrestle because we are constantly changing, and as we shift, so does our understanding of Divine presence. We wrestle because we finally see the beauty of mystery. And in fact, it is more than beautiful. It is the stuff of salvation.

MYSTERY GIVES US ROOM TO EVOLVE

I have spent most of my adult life trying to go backward without actually going backward. I've been trying to embrace my child-like faith—that posture Jesus always said was goals—while still moving forward and growing spiritually. It's tricky because it's a paradox. I used to be wary of paradox but not anymore. Now I know that mystery and paradox are besties, and I want in on the fun.

Rev. Fran Pratt, aka @TheLitanist, also happens to be my sis-in-law, colleague, and dear friend. She has long said that when we encounter a paradox, that's how we know we are close to a capital-T Truth. The wonderful thing about paradox is that there is plenty of room for evolution. We are free to become without fear of judgment. Paradox gives us space to be our full selves and to incorporate a playfulness that is essential for a joyful existence.

Each of us has a right to grow, dabble, test things out, and change our minds. You get to decide to hold things lightly along the way and pivot when needed. Which is to say you have a right to be utterly human, always changing, fully you.

In my experience, the more I've moved away from certain faith beliefs instilled within me, the more I've come back to myself. Ah, another paradox! Though my evolving has felt new (and though much of it *is* new), it is also like a consistent return. I am returning to myself. I am returning to mystery. This time, the mystery is even fuller and wider than I remembered. It's rich with paradox.

The ability to engage with all these spaces that don't make perfect sense may not feel useful at first glance. But don't get it twisted: this is our training ground for an eyes-wide-open kind of living.

MYSTERY GIVES US CAPACITY FOR HARD THINGS

Growing up, I lacked the space, permission, and language to share my realities, especially as they related to my brown experience. Sharing them in this book is a healing practice for me. But it is also a practice in vulnerability, knowing some will resonate and others will not.

In all honesty, the people pleaser in me is haunted by fears of criticism. Yet this is the work. *My work.* Learning to trust myself and listen to my intuition. Coming to believe that the Spirit of God dwells within me and learning to live like it consistently. Becoming grounded in the truth of who I am, even as I inevitably grow and evolve beyond the offering in this book.

But this is all of our work too. Because life is just a series of becoming again and again. This is exactly why we need mystery. We need room to do our becoming, and we need to move over and make room for others to do their becoming as well. We all need space to evolve. Space to wrestle. Space to get it wrong. Mystery gives us the room we need, allowing us to lean into the truth that there are few hard-and-fast rules in the process of accessing our fullness. Each of our playbooks will look different. There is no formula.

So the gift of choosing mystery is *room*. It is the capacity we need to engage the hard realities of life. It is certainly not an easy task, but it is steady. And steady is more valuable anyway.

Every time we face hard things, our stamina for discomfort expands. We aren't interested in unnecessary suffering. We aren't interested in pushing through. But we are interested in forward movement. So we move through our realities, facing them head on instead of sidestepping the difficult seasons, feelings, or experiences. Because there is no good alternative that doesn't require all of ourselves. Mystery is our path to authenticity.

MYSTERY SETS US FREE

Mystery requires more of our time, energy, and surrender than the status quo. Most of all, mystery requires us to do our own work . . . forever. We are committing to a life in the liminal space, in the nuance, in the paradox. It is tricky. It is complicated. It is layered. But we lean in anyway. We trust that with enough practice, our once-weak muscles will become strong. Our capacity will increase. Our ability to live in the tension will expand. Freedom is in sight.

Even outside of writing this book, I have a deep fear of being misunderstood. I often leave conversations and interactions in a ball of anxiety, worried about everything I said and did. I want people to see me for who I know I am. But this is not always possible, and what's more, it simply doesn't matter most of the time.

Although it's a beautiful thing to be seen and known for the truth of who we are, I'm learning that our truth shines brightest when we stop expending energy trying to be understood. In fact, wisdom is often found in seeking the opposite. May we seek to be misunderstood by becoming consistent with the truth of who we are.

We do this anytime we set up boundaries that prioritize our well-being and lay down people-pleasing. We do it when we are mindful of others without causing harm to ourselves. We do it when we care deeply about the collective and take action, without the need to be martyrs of suffering.

We choose wellness over productivity and allow rest to be our resistance. We make choices rooted not in the opinions of others but in the fullness of our *imago Dei*. Our actions reflect a deep knowing and love for ourselves. We understand that this flow benefits everyone around us.

In posturing ourselves this way, we will inevitably be misunderstood. We will be called flighty, selfish, insensitive. Assumptions will be made about us that are not true. Take heart. Trust in the paradox. We are in proximity to our deepest authenticity.

Stepping into mystery helps us understand that while there are always difficult choices to be made and unpaved paths to walk on, we have broken open the part of ourselves that was closed off to all we cannot fathom or do not yet understand. In this way, we can find a level of peace with all things.

This brings us close to yet another mysterious and paradoxical truth: that untethering and connecting can happen all at once. When we engage mystery, we are connecting to the rest of creation more deeply, even as we unbind ourselves from the rigid expectations of others.

I've spent most of my life trying to claw my way out of the liminal space I existed in. I didn't understand how I could truly belong anywhere otherwise. But living in the in-between has been my home, and I can see the beauty of this home now. It has been a training ground for walking the tightrope of nuance all along.

May we find a home with each other in this mystery. It is not easy work, but it is absolutely worth the investment. Because the more our capacity expands, the more we realize the tight-rope is actually a bridge. We are on a bridge connecting people and ideas. We've moved from *doing* healing to *being* healing. This is the freedom we were meant to embody.

13

Step into
EMBODIMENT

BODY PRAYER

One summer, I wrote a curriculum on prayer along with my copastors, Fran and Matthew. We called it *Full Spectrum: Exploring the Wide World of Spiritual Practice,* and over the years, we have used it to help broaden our community's experience with prayer.

One June evening, during a *Full Spectrum* small group, Fran led us in an ancient contemplative practice known as body prayer. Together, we stood outside in a circle on the grass, many of us opting to go barefooted. Fran guided us to move our arms in a repetitive motion. We began with our hands at our waists, followed by a prayer pose, then open arms, low to high, and finally we crossed our arms at our chests.

The movements felt strange at first, and I'm sure the nearby neighbors thought us an interesting sight. But in the summer silence, we repeated the motions over and over again. It became an experience that felt communal and deeply personal at the same time.

As I moved my body, images of Jann and my grandma came to the forefront of my mind. The closeness I felt to them, both emotionally and spiritually, nearly startled me, but I continued. Hands at my waist held out. Prayer pose. Open arms. Closed to my chest. It was the start of the month of June—the month both of these incredible women had died.

Even though their deaths were years apart, I felt connected to each of them in this moment of prayer. And even though time had passed since their transitions, I felt a fresh pang of grief wash over me unexpectedly. It came and went in waves as I continued the motions. And both of their faces became clearer in my mind.

I could see Jann's radiant smile, the stars in her eyes. The way she looked at me as if I was someone special. As if she held a secret close—the secret of my own *imago Dei*. As if she knew it was only a matter of time until I discovered it, and as if that thought tickled her.

And I could see my grandmother at her kitchen window in our tiny town. The natural light pouring into that simple space. I could see her looking out—always in that same spot—as if she was waiting for something that would never come. To look at her was to gaze upon pent-up ambition mixed with bitterness and a fierce beauty.

I might remind you that I was experiencing all this in a circle of silent sojourners. Faces were physically surrounding me, but it was these long-lost faces that continued coming to me again and again. Each set of motions felt like an invitation to let them in.

Every time I raised my arms, my spirit invited in the grief. As I crossed them to my chest, my spirit held the grief so tight, so close. When my arms lowered and opened up, it felt as if I was letting it go. It felt like my spirit was speaking. The Spirit of God in me was making space for this grief, giving me room to hold it close and honor it. And then ultimately let it go.

I continued to move through these motions, tears stinging my eyes. This physical experience of grief was painful but also oddly comforting and somehow hopeful. The letting-go motion was an empowering reminder. To grieve, yes. To know the loss, without a doubt. But also to simply *be*—to embody all the beauty I had seen from these women.

I thought to myself, *As long as I'm still here, they are still here. And my daughter, she'll know them through the stories I tell her, but also in the ways they carry on through me.* This was quite a revelation for me. And it was revealed to me through my body and specifically through the physical act of praying with all of myself.

WE ARE DISEMBODIED

To be a faith leader is to regularly bear witness to suffering, and a worldwide pandemic is no exception. Since March of 2020, I've watched as a collective pendulum swung harshly between societal despair and personal crisis in and around my community. Back and forth it swung, creating an ever-present sense of dread and palpable anxiety.

Early on, many people were able to pause aspects of their usual lives and rhythms, but at no point was anyone lucky enough to pause their circumstances. Everyone who was lonely became lonelier. Everyone who was depressed became more depressed. Everyone who financially struggled continued to struggle. Tragedies continued cropping up, even while families lost loved ones to COVID-19.

It was all too much and still is. One thing this *too-muchness* has revealed is the deep disconnect we have with our bodies. For me, so much is happening in our world, along with the realities of my own life, that I'm often in a heightened state of anxiety or a low mood. This constant stress has taken a toll on my body. I'm more tired, achier, more prone to my immune system crashing. I'm noticing that I physically can't push through taxing situations like I used to.

My body is carrying too much. *Our bodies* are carrying too much. And I am convinced we have no choice but to make changes. We must learn better ways of treating ourselves, one another, and the creation-home we share. We begin with the bodies we live in.

This is difficult work because we've mostly been taught to be suspicious of embodiment. The Christian tradition has used its ideologies to pit us against our own bodies. It has taken a dualistic posture, glorifying the spiritual and demonizing the physical. And it has used sacred text to teach us that our bodies shouldn't be trusted. So not only are we told that we cannot trust our hearts, but we are also given a praxis for living that detaches us from our physical selves.

Goodness! No wonder so many of us live our lives disconnected from our bodies. No wonder we have unhealthy, shame-filled relationships with work, food, body image, and sex. On top of this, we already carry some level of trauma in our bodies. Trauma from our own tragic experiences and from physical, mental, emotional, and spiritual exhaustion. But also trauma from historical wounds: pain from our parents and the pain of our ancestors.

It's like we've got Good Friday trauma living in us, and we need (quite literally) the healing and wholeness of a bodily resurrection. We need to breathe new life into the relationship we have with our bodies. We need to unbind our hearts, minds, *and bodies* from the unwanted paradigms that have been handed to us. And we need to dismantle and throw out many of the ways we've been conditioned to perceive other bodies too.

Think about it. Women are taught that our bodies were made for two things: childbearing and the sexual pleasure of men. We are taught we don't have agency over our bodies. We are told to submit without question, and we are blamed when crappy theology is used to justify violence toward us.

We are taught to fear and hate queer, trans, and gender-nonconforming bodies. Violence toward these bodies is an epidemic. We are taught to deny basic human dignity to fat bodies or disabled bodies. We are taught that Black and brown bodies are inferior and untrustworthy and must be policed and subdued. We see the proof in our streets and at our borders.

Disembodied theological roots have nourished the political and social structures that make these things so. This matters to each of us because we are all connected, even if we don't always embrace this connection. We need each other to understand our personal and collective traumas. We need our inner work to expand outside of ourselves in order to put a collective dent in our embrace of embodiment.

EMBODIED INTUITION

Many women, myself included, can speak of a feminine wound that goes deeper than their individual self. Many people of color, especially Black and Indigenous people in our country, can speak of the generational wound they inherited. It is a grief of the ages that sits on our shoulders, unwanted yet ours to bear.

When I consider my grandmother's story, I begin to understand that it is my story too. I know her struggles; I feel her shame. And even though she's physically gone, I understand the aches she carried in her body.

Nearly every night as I'm falling asleep, my eyes begin to water so much that I must wipe unexplained tears away. And every time this happens, I am reminded of her at that kitchen table by the window, wiping her inexplicably watery eyes in the same way. I know without a doubt—*in my body*—that we carry the same stories and traumas. And the definition of intuition tells me that I don't have to logically explain this to anyone. I know it. My body knows it. We are connected.

So I'm telling you that whatever we need to heal from— individually and collectively—we ought to prioritize. Because our bodies will carry it otherwise, and our children's will too. So we heal for the sake of our past: our ancestors; for the sake of our present: ourselves; and for the sake of our future: our children and all of creation. And I am convinced that this healing is incomplete without an embodied intuition.

We have an innate need to connect with our bodies in such a way that we know what they are trying to tell us at any given moment. To loop our physical experience into our mental, emotional, and spiritual processes. Consistently listening to, trusting, and honoring the messages our body sends us is to embrace an embodied intuition.

Tuning in to our embodied intuition has spiritual relevance. When we develop an embodied posture, we inevitably find deeper Divine connection. This connection to our *imago Dei* helps us understand who we are as whole people. This is power. It helps us identify where we need change, where we need evolution, where we need shifting. This is power. It helps us understand the healing we seek, which gives us clarity and direction. This is power.

The more we lean into this posture, the more we understand why there cannot be a prepackaged recipe for all of us. The work of embodied intuition is not a meal kit. It is not convenient, and there are no exact measurements preprepped for us. Instead, we are planting and growing our own food here. We are doing the harvesting. And we are cooking things up, depending on what's in season.

So the work of embodiment is fluid, constantly changing from moment to moment, day to day, season to season. This is why embodied intuition is a much-needed spiritual discipline. It takes consistency and practice. When we do the work, we become people who know how to listen to God, and the more we listen, the more we recognize God within us, God alive in our bodies.

The natural result is that we begin to live more intuitively. We become less concerned with time, less concerned with production, and less concerned with the expectations of others. We make decisions, navigate relationships, and care for ourselves from this place. In other words, we learn to live in sync with our Spirit, as intended.

I know, I know. A checklist would have been easier. I don't have that for you. But remember? We have what we need already: our own self. Our own willingness to do the work. And the power of our *imago Dei* within us. *Spirit of God* within us. We must learn how to listen. We must.

Enter the necessity of ritual.

THE POWER OF RITUAL

A couple of months into the worldwide pandemic, a dear family in my congregation experienced the tragic death of their three-year-old son, Ezra Arnold Leschber. Words cannot express how painful Ezzy's loss was for his family and the communities who love him. As a mom, my heart ached even just attempting to fathom the grief. There are no words. There is no comfort. The best we can do sometimes is bring our love via a hot meal. A physical offering promising something deeper: the commitment to walk with them in the brutally hard. Indeed, in our church, the meal train has become one of our most sacred rituals.

So on a blazing-hot June evening, I headed to their doorstep with a meal in tow. Because this family was newer to our congregation, I was not used to the particular drive that led to their home. Living in one of the fastest-growing counties in the country, I am used to passing a lot of city roads, new neighborhoods, business complexes, grocery stores, and restaurants.

But my drive to this family's home took me out into the country. It was also somewhat of a long drive from my house, so I found myself with plenty of time to think. That night was the eve of my grandma's death anniversary. I always mark her day with a ritual using sunflowers. My grandmother loved sunflowers, proven by her sunflower placemats and blankets and anything else with the theme she could own. And so we always have them on the day of her birth, as well as on the day of her death. And I always think of her when I see them.

As I was driving, I wondered which store along the way might have some sunflowers. I felt an urgency to find them. I was so in my thoughts that I became unaware of my surroundings. But then I rounded a corner and found myself driving down a road I had never been on before. The road was lined on both sides with endless fields of Texas sunflowers. It was so overwhelming, I could not believe it.

Suddenly, I was reminded in body and spirit of our oneness. I felt a deep connection to the Leschber family. So close to their home, I felt a shared grief with them. I also felt connected to my grandmother and my family. And, simultaneously, I felt connected to the earth and to God. In that moment—that collision of pain and beauty—I sensed a *bodily* reminder that we are one.

It was a ritual moment I did not create myself, but I recognized it as such.

The following morning on my grandmother's day, I loaded up my family, and we made the long drive once more. Standing in the heat of the brilliant sun, we talked about her life. We bore witness to our grief and love. My daughter laid down some painted rocks she had made for the occasion. My father helped me snip a few flowers to take home. Three generations stood in her presence and power. No explanation required. We created the ritual, and it led us to ourselves in some small way.

The more we are able to name the rituals we already do and make meaning out of them, the more creativity we tap into that inspires us to create the rituals we need. Oh, sure, our bodies can get along just fine without ritual, but trust me. We are all the better for it if we make the space in our lives for a spirituality that engages all of our senses. This is what ritual does.

Ritual is the bridge between our Spirit-intuition and our bodily intuition. It is the place where we meld and merge all of ourselves. And this is exactly it: we are meant to live with all of ourselves. Not one part of us gets left behind.

A PRAYER FOR EMBODIMENT

May we honor our bodies. May we take the time to breathe, stretch, be still, and assess how we feel.

May we understand the deeper truths our bodies tell us: when we need rest, discipline, or play. Where we need healing.

May our bodies remind us that the Divine dwells here. And may we believe it without the need for conscious reasoning, permission, or approval.

May we develop an embodied intuition: God is with us, in us, around us, among us. Even as the earth groans. Even in these times of collective chaos.

We are stepping into our power, and we are taking our bodies with us.

14

Step into
YOUR POWER

REVIVAL

*A gathering of dusty, deflated balloons has
floated into my room
at the precise moment I am thinking about regret.*

*I am grieving my unasked questions,
the untold stories, unshared wisdom of my
abuelita.*

*If only she were here now,
if only I had woken up sooner!*

*The sunken balloons are hovering on the edge
of life,
reminding me of what is no longer possible.*

Suddenly, the door swings open,
jolting me into the present moment.

My little daughter is coming in;
she is planting kisses on my nose.

Roaring with laughter, she runs through
the balloons,
willing them back to life, if only just for
a moment.

Now bursts of blue and green are exploding in
the air;
she is reviving them!

A flash of recognition surges through my body
at the sight of my daughter's wild and
defiant smile.

I have glimpsed my grandmother's Spirit,
and all is not lost.

The ache of regret is painful,
the dull twinge in my gut from time lost is fresh.

But she is still here, healing me,
reviving me.

OUR MATRIARCH

I remember dancing at a family wedding many years ago. I was having so much fun that night out on the dance floor surrounded by my people, a rarity since my dad and his siblings are split among several states. I looked over at our gathering of tables in the corner where my grandmother sat, her power effortlessly radiating as usual.

As she watched us dance with an air of nonchalance, I went over to her. I was curious about what she was thinking, and so I bent down low and let her speak her mind in my ear. She gestured to the dance floor, and with that mischievous glint in her eyes, she said, "See all this? You're all here because of me."

Truly, she was our matriarch. My connection to her remains strong because so much of her is still undeniably present. If ever I doubt this, I need only to observe my daughter for a few moments. Her nature, that glint in her eye. The way her energy commands the room. She is like a healed version of my grandma wreaking glorious havoc on the world.

I'd bet my sister and cousins could say the same of their children in so many ways. It's true for us, as well as for my oldest sister, Angela—her namesake. And it's true for all our parents too. We are connected. When we pay attention, we see that our traumas and triumphs are wrapped up together. Naming the stories of those who came before us can be a beautiful part of claiming our power. Understanding my grandmother's inner landscape has helped me make sense of my own.

My grandma was born on All Saints Day, and she died on Pentecost Sunday. In fact, there is no better way to describe her contrary, irreverent nature than the fact that she came into this world on a day honoring the dead and died on a day commemorating the living Spirit poured out on the early Christians. What's more, her name translated to *angel of the saints*, and while Angela De Los Santos surely believed in God, she could hardly be described as religiously devout.

Surely my grandma's religious disinterest began with her mother, who never attended Mass until her old age. According to my grandma, her mother was mean, coldhearted, and unloving. She was abusive and neglectful, ultimately driving my grandma to marry young and quickly take off to Chicago with her new husband and little support.

So when her mother died, my grandma did not grieve. She said of her death, "*I went to see her to honor her. Respect her. But I did not miss her. I did not know her.*" She never spoke of her mother with any deep emotion. Instead, her feelings toward her mom were always framed as a matter of objective truth.

My great-grandmother was consistent in pushing anybody and everybody away. Even on her deathbed, she would turn away the priest who would daily come to offer communion, saying, "*Get out of here! I don't want to see you.*" Reflecting on this, my decidedly not devout grandma said, "*She didn't even have time for God.*"

I think my grandma was on to something when she took notice of this. But perhaps a better way to think about it is this: instead of not having time for God, my great-grandmother did not have *space* for God. I know very few things about my great-grandmother, but everything I do know tells me her life was utterly tragic.

Perhaps trauma treated my great-grandma the same way it treats the rest of us: seeping into our lives, sending us the worst messages about ourselves and the world. Maybe trauma filled up her capacities with untruths until there was no space for God stuff. And though her actions were her own responsibility, perhaps the lack of capacity wasn't her fault. Maybe we can relate to literally not having space for Divine love and goodness sometimes. Maybe we know what it's like to feel sick from trauma, tragedy, stress, and circumstances.

What if we shifted our focus from making *time* for healing practices to focusing on making *space* for them? We make space whenever we step outside of the paradigms that perpetuate our trauma-informed scripts. We make space when we step into healthy paradigms that are rooted in our *imago Dei*.

Trauma, shame, fear, and grief fill up our capacities, and the work of healing is our medicine. Our lack of healing keeps us separated from our fullness, but the medicine strengthens us, creating space for Divine presence. Waking us up to the power already within us. We should take the medicine. We should do the work.

GOOD FORM

I've recently taken up the hobby of wakesurfing. When you are learning to get up on the board, you start out by holding on to a rope. Once you are up, you use your body to stay in the wake. Once you know how to stay in the wake, you can let go of the rope and surf. I did not grow up comfortable in the water, so learning this sport has not been intuitive for me.

There are countless things you have to remember in learning how to wakesurf. Sometimes it helps to have someone watch from the back of the boat, shouting out tips: "Keep your knees bent. Don't pull on the rope. Keep your feet light and your weight on your toes. Keep your front shoulder in. Stay low."

But here's the thing: once you get in the sweet spot of the wave and you can finally let go of the rope, something inevitably starts to click within you. Your body begins to understand what it feels like to be there. And you don't have to do so much thinking, remembering, and questioning in order to keep your form.

Stepping into our power is like this. The more we do our inner work of letting go of what's harmful, listening to body and spirit—and honoring what we hear—the more it clicks. The more we move into an intuitive space where we *know*, beyond words, what it feels like. Our practice becomes the continued work of committing that knowledge to memory.

As automatic as muscle memory, we can know what it means to stand in our power. We will always benefit from authentic, healthy support. And there will always be the need to adjust, improve, and continue learning. But over time, we realize we don't need people shouting instructions at us. We get to a point where we can let go of our metaphorical rope. We can trust our bodies, hearts, and spirits to know what to do. No one can find the sweet spot *for us*. No one can experience what it feels like to reclaim our intuition *for us*. This is why we don't need anyone else's authority to stand in our power. It's up to us to keep good form.

PINK PANTIES

When I was a kid, I got teased for being brown. In response, I did everything I could to *not* stand out among my peers. Then one day on the playground, my dress inched up while playing, revealing my pink underwear. A couple of boys noticed and teased me for it. For what seemed like eternity, they shouted, "*Pink panties!*" anytime they saw me. It was humiliating.

It's so ridiculous, but after that, I wouldn't wear pink for years. Even after getting married, I can remember telling my in-laws, "Anything but pink" when they asked about my favorite colors for future gift ideas. I didn't wear pink for so long that I actually forgot why I even hated it.

Regardless, for years, I would wear dark clothing to try to not stand out. If I arrived late anywhere, I would get so much anxiety that I would be unable to walk into the crowded room. I have terrible posture from years of slouching because to stand up straight and tall felt too much like standing out.

But now I know better. Now I understand that a good posture is one that allows no part of ourselves to be neglected. From our voices and experiences, and even to our bodies, a good inner posture will compel us to celebrate our existence rather than stifle it. Somewhere along my healing journey, I wrote these words:

> *I'll speak my truth as if I had no choice*
> *Without apology, shoulders back, chin up*
> *I will use my brown woman's voice.*

So. Every pair of wild earrings I wear now is my act of resistance to the harmful messaging I absorbed as a child. Every
tube of bold lipstick announces that healed and whole Aurelia is
here to stay. And every shade of bright pink I own lays claim to
my power. I have seen my *imago Dei*, and I won't unsee her. The
more I see *imago Dei* in me, the more I see it in you. In us.

So much beauty.

TOUGH AS NAILS

Once in seminary, I had a professor call me up after class. I
didn't know him well, but he was beloved at our school for his
quick wit and warm yet no-nonsense demeanor. In his thick
Texas drawl, he said, *"Something about you reminds me of my
grandmother. Tiny little thing, but she was tough as nails."*

I still chuckle thinking about this. It was our first real interaction, but it wasn't the first time I'd received such a comment. I
still remember my now-husband sharing what our mutual friend
relayed to him when he inquired about me in college: *"Oh,
that Aurelia, she'll tell you like it is."* I've been told I'm fiery and
feisty and that I don't have a filter. And all of it makes me proud
because it reminds me that even in the worst of times, I've never
truly had a nature prone to shrinking.

In so many ways, I've always been Angela's granddaughter.
Sweet or nice were never her identifiers. She was a spitfire full
of personality. You had to meet her only once to know it. She
didn't take any bullshit. She was brutally honest, often to a fault.
Yet she could muster up a lie in an instant if she wanted to and
never feel ashamed about it. When I was a kid, I called her "the

mean grandma" because if I'm honest, she scared the crap out of me.

These are the kinds of things my family talks about with a laugh, but the truth is so much of who she was came from a place of pain. My grandmother endured so much as a child: The death of her father when she was young. In many ways, a social outcast in her community. Poverty, neglect, abuse. A mother who was not present. A husband who would ultimately abandon her as well.

I think about her childhood and how her mother used to have my grandma go to the white neighborhoods and steal butter and milk from the milkman's truck. And I think about how almost daily, I ask my own daughter not to waste her milk after having her cereal. My grandma's constant litany of "*remember where you came from*" still rings in my ears.

This access to milk. This access to healing. My grandma didn't have the same kind of access to any of it the way I do. She wasn't perfect. She doled out a generous amount of the harm she inherited, and her children suffered for it. Still, in her own way, she carved a pathway to healing for them. She created a different reality with new possibilities for her kids. And her children have done the same exponentially for my generation. Our access to healing is even greater than they could have dreamed up for us. I won't be wasteful of their sacrifices.

INCHING OUR WAY TOWARD HEALING

Every year, leading up to my grandmother's birthday on Dia de los Muertos, I light candles. I put up photos. I set out food.

I build an *ofrenda*, and I share stories of our ancestors with my daughter. The past comes, and it joins us in the present moment. Offering us love. Offering us guidance.

When we look only ahead, we begin to wonder if we can endure everything we're facing in these times. But when we look back, we are reminded that our efforts have always been a continuation of those who came before us. We may carry the trauma of our ancestors' realities on our backs, but we also carry their power. It is a tough-as-nails kind of power, full of all the grit of those who came before us, making our way a bit easier.

Generation to generation, we are inching our way toward healing. As we inch along, we begin to understand the urgency of naming our stories. We begin to see how our own inner work stands alongside the support of our ancestors and sacred communities. It is like our own holy trinity working miracles in our lives. What was dead can be alive. What was buried can be resurrected.

It is from this place of hard-won hope where we reclaim our intuition and step into the birthright of our God-given power. To do so is our ultimate act of resistance. This refusal to receive any narrative other than the one we write for ourselves is what it means to be fully alive.

The timeline we are living in is wild and chaotic, making it difficult to look ahead with confidence. When an unknown future overwhelms my present reality, looking back offers the grounding perspective I need. Once again, I am reminded of who I am. I am reminded of what I know to be true about me. About us.

We are children of God. The stuff of Spirit swirls around within us. We are culminations of our ancestors' stories. We are story bearers. Our existence is holy, and our healing is their healing too. For those who came before us, for all who will come after. And, yes, even for ourselves, may it be so.

Closing Words

My dear friend,

This was only a nudge.
A friendly reminder
of what was always true.

Intuition
Power
Imago Dei.

Yours, yours, yours.

Acknowledgments

We tend to write tributes for our loved ones
only after they've died

to honor their memory
to express our affection and gratitude
to preserve their life with pretty words.

This is exactly what I did for my grandma, that feisty and
glorious soul,
and to be quite honest, I'm not sure it's what she would
have wanted.

My grandma used to love to tell us, "Shit happens, and then
you die."
She always referred to her belongings as "junk."
She insisted on not having photos of her husband because
"he's dead," she would say.

It was as if in her own harsh way, she was more interested in
living solely in the present.
It wasn't just preference; it was survival.

So this is what I will do:
I will live in the now.
I will hold things that don't matter lightly.

And I will write tributes of thanks for the ones I love
while they are still here to hear them:

To Alicia. My sister, *thank you*. You've held my hand in countless ways, from childhood to the writing of these stories. When I felt afraid or unsure, you were always there. Then and now. Chapter after chapter. My stories are your stories, and yours are mine. This book is for us.

To Kyndall. The ultimate spacemaker. You've made way for me to preach, lead, use my voice, and hone my creativity. For connecting me with your editor at Broadleaf Books, and for all the spaces you've created for me over the last decade, *thank you*.

To Lyle. As usual, you have been unwavering in your support of me. You've shared in every excitement. Insisted we celebrate every single milestone. You've cleared your calendar time and again to make way for my dreams. You've held down our fort and cared for our girl so I could write. I love you. *Thank you*.

To Brandie, Heather, Jana, Kayla, and Naomi. Your love, support, and blessing have been my solid ground from start to finish. Endless gratitude—a deep well of it! For each of you. *Thank you*.

To Fran and Matthew. My copastors and cocreators of sacred art. This book is a canon of my beliefs, many of which have been nurtured in community and conversation with you. You showed up for me in big ways so I could complete this project. *Thank you*.

To Brittany. This book was birthed in the dream spaces we created. Our collaborations have given me more courage and growth than I could have imagined. *Thank you*.

To Bethany. There was no waking up without you. When I consider my healing, there you are, offering unlimited love, patience, and guidance. *Muchas gracias, hermana.*

To Anna Swisher. You told me I should write a book, and you kept telling me until I did it! For believing I have something to say, always checking in, and being a most sacred wise woman in my life. *Thank you.*

To Peace of Christ Church. It is a rarity to freely and honestly navigate the things of God within a healthy faith community. You beautiful people have given me endless space, endless love, and endless acceptance. *Thank you.*

To Erin Szczerba, Rev. Zach Dawes Jr., Dr. David Holley, Mark Johansson, Amanda Bowen, Jana Muñoz, and all our leadership at Peace. For creating sabbatical space for me to write. For prioritizing our pastors' rest and care, now and in the days to come. *Thank you.*

To my auntie Lisa. For so thoughtfully recording interviews with your mom, my grandma. Her stories were a gift as I worked on the final chapter of this book. *Gracias, Auntie.*

To James, Lauren, and Tia. Your love has gone with me all these years. As I wrote down these stories, gratitude rose up for our friendship. Kindreds forever. *Thank you.*

To Greg Garrett. For a lifechanging phone call. For lending your wisdom to this first-time writer. You were a catalyst for this book in so many ways. *Thank you.*

To Rev. Robin Drake. I learned about *imago Dei* in seminary, but something about it sunk deep in my soul when I heard your sermon "Waking Up Woman" in 2017. *Thank you.*

To Karen González. For your time and invaluable advice early on, which absolutely shaped my writing process, *Gracias, hermana.*

To Lisa Kloskin. My editor. For taking such care with my words and ideas. For being available and sensitive to the personal nature of this writing journey. I really enjoyed working together, and just for the record, you are still my favorite name to appear in my inbox! *Thank you.*

To the entire team at Broadleaf working behind the scenes to get this book published. To Marcie Lawrence for creating a cover that embodies the spirit of this book. And to each and every friend who was willing to endorse *A Brown Girl's Epiphany,* my endless gratitude goes with you. *Thank you.*

Finally, to the land that sustained me, body and soul. To its original stewards, the Jumanos, Tonkawa, Comanche, Lipan Apache, and Coahuiltecan tribes. And to the sunrise, my constant companion. For greeting me each morning in all four seasons as I wrote. *Thank you.*

Like our stories, collaboration is a pathway to healing. This book is incomplete without these acknowledgments. *Thank you, thank you, thank you.*

NOTES

Chapter 1

1   Fr. Richard Rohr, "The Dualistic Mind" (January 29, 2017). https://cac.org/the-dualistic-mind-2017-01-29/.

Chapter 6

2   Wynn McGregor, *The Way of the Child* (Nashville: Upper Room Books, 2006), 228.

Chapter 8

3   Gloria Anzaldúa, *Borderlands/La Frontera: The New Mestiza*, 4th ed. (San Francisco: Aunt Lute Books, 2007), 81.

Chapter 9

4   Matthew 18:1–3, New Revised Standard Version.

Chapter 11

5   Kyndall Rae Rothaus, *Thy Queendom Come* (Minneapolis: Broadleaf Books, 2021), 13.

Chapter 12

6   Pádraig Ó. Tuama, *In the Shelter: Finding a Home in the World* (Minneapolis: Broadleaf Books, 2015), 18.